Delish

JUST FOUR
ingredients
Fast!

Delish

JUST FOUR
ingredients

Fast!

HEARST BOOKS
New York

contents

Brunch

There's no hurry—turn off the alarm and relax. It's the weekend so put on your slippers, brew some coffee, and settle in for a leisurely brunch with family and friends.

pineapple, carrot, and beet juice

¼ small pineapple,
  peeled, sliced thickly
2 medium carrots
1 small red beet, chopped
1 tablespoon lime juice

1 Push pineapple, carrots, and beet through juice extractor into glass. Stir in 2 tablespoons water and lime juice.

prep time 5 minutes **serves** 1
nutritional count per serving
0.3g total fat (0g saturated fat);
105 cal; 20.7g carbohydrate;
2.8g protein; 3.5g fiber

apple, carrot, and ginger juice

3 medium carrots
1 stalk celery, trimmed
1 medium apple, quartered
¾-inch piece fresh ginger,
  peeled

1 Push carrots, celery, apple, and ginger through juice extractor into glass. Stir in 2 tablespoons water.

prep time 5 minutes **serves** 1
nutritional count per serving
0.4g total fat (0g saturated fat);
128 cal; 25.6g carbohydrate;
2.1g protein; 5.7g fiber

tip This juice is a mega-healthy boost for your body. Pineapple has anti-inflammatory properties and helps the body digest protein; carrots are packed with vitamins A and C; beets are reputed to be one of the best liver-cleansing vegetables. Cheers!

pineapple, carrot, and beet juice

tip Ginger not only cleans, stimulates, and rejuvenates the digestive system, it also adds a refreshing zing to the sweetness of the apple and carrot.

apple, carrot, and ginger juice

tip To make this a more filling breakfast smoothie, you could add a few spoonfuls of toasted muesli.

berry smoothie

tip A frappé is best made just before serving because the thick, creamy texture will subside and separate if it stands for too long.

watermelon, berry, and mint frappé

berry smoothie

8 ounces strawberries
½ cup blueberries
1 cup skim milk
¾ cup low-fat berry yogurt

prep time 5 minutes **serves** 2
nutritional count per serving
0.5g total fat (0.2g saturated fat);
170 cal; 26.9g carbohydrate;
12.2g protein; 3.4g fiber

1 Blend ingredients until smooth.

You can use either fresh or frozen blueberries in the smoothie.

watermelon, berry, and mint frappé

14 ounces seedless
  watermelon, chopped
  coarsely
4 ounces strawberries
1 tablespoon lime juice
¼ cup fresh mint leaves

prep time 5 minutes **serves** 2
nutritional count per serving
0.3g total fat (0g saturated fat);
40 cal; 7.1g carbohydrate;
1.5g protein; 1.4g fiber

1 Blend or process watermelon, berries, juice, and mint with about 20 ice cubes until smooth.

muesli and honey yogurt

⅓ cup yogurt

1 teaspoon honey

⅓ cup toasted muesli
(granola)

2 tablespoons dried
cranberries

prep time 5 minutes **serves** 1
nutritional count per serving
6.4g total fat (2.6g saturated fat);
346 cal; 60.9g carbohydrate;
8.8g protein; 4.8g fiber

1 Combine yogurt and honey in small bowl.
Combine muesli and cranberries in another
small bowl.
2 Layer yogurt mixture and muesli in
serving glass. Serve immediately.

oatmeal

1½ cups rolled oats

½ cup milk

2 tablespoons superfine sugar

1 teaspoon ground cinnamon

prep + cook time 10 minutes
serves 4
nutritional count per serving
4.1g total fat (1.3g saturated fat);
187 cal; 31.4g carbohydrate;
4.7g protein; 2.4g fiber

1 Combine oats and 3½ cups hot water in
medium saucepan over medium heat; cook,
stirring, about 5 minutes or until oatmeal is
thick and creamy.
2 Stir in milk. Serve oatmeal sprinkled with
combined sugar and cinnamon.

yogurt with dried fruit and coconut

2 tablespoons finely chopped
  dried apricots
2 tablespoons finely chopped
  raisins
2 teaspoons desiccated
  coconut
¾ cup yogurt

1 Combine fruit and coconut in small bowl. Place yogurt in serving bowl; sprinkle the apricot mixture over the top.

prep time 5 minutes **serves** 1
nutritional count per serving
6.4g total fat (4.5g saturated fat);
323 cal; 51.6g carbohydrate;
12.2g protein; 3.7g fiber

ricotta and banana on toast

2 tablespoons low-fat
  ricotta cheese
2 slices rye bread, toasted
2 small bananas,
  sliced thickly
1 teaspoon honey

1 Divide cheese between toast slices; top with banana then drizzle the honey over.

prep + cook time 10 minutes
serves 2
nutritional count per serving
2.9g total fat (1.3g saturated fat);
231 cal; 40.6g carbohydrate;
7.7g protein; 5g fiber

cheesy corn on rye

11-ounce can corn kernels,
   rinsed, drained
2 tablespoons low-fat
   ricotta cheese
1½ ounces baby spinach
   leaves
2 slices rye bread, toasted

prep + cook time 5 minutes
serves 2
nutritional count per serving
4.4g total fat (1.7g saturated fat);
268 cal; 42.2g carbohydrate;
10.6g protein; 7.2g fiber

1 Heat corn in medium bowl in microwave
oven on HIGH (100%) for about 30 seconds;
stir in cheese and spinach.
2 Serve toast topped with corn mixture.

bran and cranberry muesli

1 cup rolled oats
¾ cup bran flakes
¼ cup dried cranberries
½ cup fresh blueberries

prep time 5 minutes **serves** 2
nutritional count per serving
6.1g total fat (2.2g saturated fat);
346 cal; 60.3g carbohydrate;
8g protein; 9.5g fiber

1 Combine oats, bran, and cranberries in
small bowl to make muesli mixture.
2 Serve muesli topped with berries

Serve with milk or yogurt.

Store remaining muesli in an airtight container.

cheesy corn on rye

tip Low-fat ricotta is widely available in containers from the cheese section of most supermarkets.

bran and cranberry muesli

tip Dried cranberries, high in vitamin C and antioxidants, are a tart and delicious addition to this already healthy brunch.

tip Silicone muffin pans are perfect for making little egg bakes like these, as you can easily flip the bacon and egg pie out of the mold without sticking. If you don't have a silicone pan, you should grease the pan holes well before adding the bacon and egg, otherwise you might have a little trouble getting them out.

egg and bacon pies

tip You could also use Worcestershire sauce instead of balsamic vinegar, if you like.

tomato and egg muffin

egg and bacon pies

2 strips bacon, cooked and
  chopped finely
2 eggs
2 slices rye bread, toasted
1 small tomato,
  chopped finely

prep + cook time 20 minutes
serves 2
nutritional count per serving
7.2g total fat (2g saturated fat);
214 cal; 21g carbohydrate;
21g protein; 3.6g fiber

1 Preheat oven to 400°F/375°F convection.
2 Divide bacon between two ⅓-cup muffin
pan holes. Crack an egg into each hole.
Bake about 15 minutes or until egg is set.
Loosen edge of pies from pan.
3 Serve pies on toast; sprinkle the tomato
over the pies.

tomato and egg muffin

2 eggs
2 multigrain English muffins,
  split
1 small tomato, sliced thinly
2 teaspoons balsamic vinegar

prep + cook time 10 minutes
serves 2
nutritional count per serving
7.3g total fat (1.9g saturated fat);
228 cal; 24.2g carbohydrate;
14.5g protein; 3.9g fiber

1 Fry eggs in oiled medium frying pan until
cooked as you like them.
2 Meanwhile, toast muffins.
3 Divide tomato between two muffin
halves; sprinkle the vinegar over, top with
eggs, then the remaining muffin halves.

smoked salmon and mascarpone omelette

8 eggs

½ cup (4 ounces) mascarpone cheese

3½ ounces sliced smoked salmon

2 tablespoons finely chopped fresh chervil

prep + cook time 25 minutes
serves 4
nutritional count per serving
30.6g total fat (16.3g saturated fat); 358 cal; 1g carbohydrate; 20.6g protein; 0.1g fiber

1 Whisk eggs with 2 tablespoons of the cheese in medium bowl until combined.
2 Oil small 6-inch frying pan; heat over medium heat. Pour a quarter of the egg mixture into pan. Cook, tilting pan, until omelette is set.
3 Top half of the omelette with a quarter of the salmon, a quarter of the chervil, and a quarter of the remaining cheese. Fold omelette over to enclose filling; slide onto serving plate.
4 Repeat to make three more omelettes.

eggs in toast

4 thick slices white bread

1 tablespoon butter

4 eggs

2 tablespoons bottled tomato salsa

prep + cook time 15 minutes
serves 4
nutritional count per serving
11.5g total fat (5.1g saturated fat); 241 cal; 23.5g carbohydrate; 10.1g protein; 1.4g fiber

1 Cut a 3-inch circle from the center of each slice of bread. Discard center pieces (or process and freeze for ready-made bread crumbs).
2 Melt butter in large frying pan; cook bread until browned lightly on one side. Turn bread; crack one egg into the center of each piece of bread.
3 Cook, over low heat, until egg white just sets. Using spatula, gently lift toast onto serving plates. Serve with salsa.

baked eggs with prosciutto and pecorino

6 slices prosciutto, chopped finely

4 green onions, chopped finely

2/3 cup finely grated pecorino cheese

8 eggs

prep + cook time 20 minutes
serves 4
nutritional count per serving
17.7g total fat (7g saturated fat); 252 cal; 0.9g carbohydrate; 22.6g protein; 0.2g fiber

1 Preheat oven to 400°F/375°F convection. Lightly oil four ¾-cup ovenproof dishes.
2 Cook prosciutto in heated oiled medium frying pan until crisp. Add onion; cook, stirring, until onion just softens. Remove from heat; stir in half the cheese.
3 Divide prosciutto mixture among dishes; break two eggs into each dish. Bake mixture, uncovered, in oven, 5 minutes. Sprinkle remaining cheese over eggs; return to oven. Bake, uncovered, 5 minutes or until eggs are just set. Serve immediately.

scrambled eggs with asparagus

6 ounces asparagus, trimmed

4 eggs

2 tablespoons skim milk

1 small tomato, chopped finely

prep + cook time 15 minutes
serves 2
nutritional count per serving
10.6g total fat (3.2g saturated fat); 174 cal; 3g carbohydrate; 16g protein; 1.4g fiber

1 Boil, steam, or microwave asparagus until tender; drain.
2 Whisk eggs and milk in medium bowl. Cook egg mixture in oiled medium frying pan, over low heat, stirring, until almost set.
3 Serve asparagus and scrambled eggs topped with tomato.

Scrambled eggs need to be cooked and stirred gently until they are creamy and barely cooked. Overcooking will toughen them. Eat them right away or they'll become watery.

spiced plums with yogurt

2 × 30-ounce jars whole
plums
2 cinnamon sticks
6 cardamom pods
1 cup Greek-style yogurt

prep + cook time 15 minutes
serves 6
nutritional count per serving
3.4g total fat (2.1g saturated fat);
130 cal; 21.5g carbohydrate;
3g protein; 0.9g fiber

1 Drain the juice from plums into medium saucepan. Add spices to the pan; bring to a boil. Reduce heat, simmer, uncovered, 3 minutes.
2 Remove from heat. Add plums to juice mixture; cover pan, stand 10 minutes. Serve warm plums with yogurt; drizzle the juice mixture over them.

roasted rhubarb and cranberries

2 pounds rhubarb, trimmed,
chopped coarsely
¼ cup dried cranberries
¼ cup brown sugar
1 tablespoon orange juice

prep + cook time 25 minutes
serves 4
nutritional count per serving
0.6g total fat (0g saturated fat);
136 cal; 24.2g carbohydrate;
4g protein; 8.4g fiber

1 Preheat oven to 350°F/325°F convection.
2 Combine ingredients in medium shallow baking dish. Roast, uncovered, about 20 minutes or until rhubarb is just tender.

spiced plums with yogurt

tip Cardamom is a spice native to India that has a distinctive aromatic, sweetly rich flavor. It is used to flavor curries, rice dishes, sweet desserts, and cakes.

roasted rhubarb and cranberries

tip Try serving this delicious fruit dish with a few good dollops of sweetened mascarpone cheese or vanilla yogurt.

Lunch on the run

When you're rushing around in the middle of the day, don't forget about lunch. These quick and easy-to-prepare meals are ideal for packing up and eating on the go.

roast beef and coleslaw on rye

1 tablespoon creamy
  horseradish
4 slices rare roast beef
  (4 ounces)
4 slices rye bread
5 ounces prepared coleslaw

1 Sandwich horseradish, beef, and coleslaw between bread slices.

2 Cut as desired to serve.

prep time 10 minutes **serves** 2
nutritional count per serving
9.8g total fat (2.6g saturated fat);
415 cal; 51.1g carbohydrate;
25g protein; 9.7g fiber

egg and chive sandwich

2 hard-boiled eggs, halved
2 tablespoons low-fat
  ricotta cheese
2 tablespoons finely chopped
  fresh chives
4 slices rye bread

1 Place egg, cheese, and chives in medium bowl; using back of fork, crush until combined.

2 Sandwich egg mixture between bread slices. Cut as desired to serve.

prep time 5 minutes **serves** 2
nutritional count per serving
9.5g total fat (3.2g saturated fat);
330 cal; 40.4g carbohydrate;
17.1g protein; 6.1g fiber

roast beef and cole slaw on rye

egg and chive sandwich

tip Coleslaw is a great crunchy addition to sandwiches. As long as shredded cabbage is the chief ingredient, you can add just about anything else to it. Most coleslaws also have grated carrots and a mayonnaise or vinegar (or both) dressing.

tip For perfect hard boiled eggs, place eggs in salted boiling water for 7 minutes and then drain. Immediately put them in cold water and stand a few minutes before peeling. It's worth doing a few at a time so you have some on hand for sandwiches, salads, or just a simple snack.

ricotta, zucchini, and ham wrap

turkey and cranberry wrap

ricotta, zucchini, and ham wrap

2 small zucchini
¼ cup low-fat ricotta cheese
3 rye or whole wheat wraps
3 ounces shaved ham

prep + cook time 10 minutes
serves 2
nutritional count per serving
4.7g total fat (2.3g saturated fat);
212 cal; 24.1g carbohydrate;
16.1g protein; 3.7g fiber

1 Preheat sandwich press.
2 Slice zucchini lengthwise into ribbons using a vegetable peeler.
3 Divide cheese among wraps; top with zucchini and ham. Roll to enclose.
4 Toast wraps in sandwich press about 3 minutes.
5 Cut in half to serve.

turkey and cranberry wrap

2 rye or whole wheat wraps
2 tablespoons cranberry sauce
3 ounces shaved turkey
½ cup mixed salad leaves

prep time 5 minutes serves 2
nutritional count per serving
2.1g total fat (0.4g saturated fat);
203 cal; 27.6g carbohydrate;
16.7g protein; 2.5g fiber

1 Spread wraps with sauce; top with remaining ingredients. Roll to enclose.
2 Cut as desired to serve.

watermelon and berry salad

4-pound piece seedless
 watermelon
8 ounces strawberries, halved
4 ounces fresh blueberries
¼ cup loosely packed fresh
 mint leaves

1 Using melon baller, cut out watermelon balls.

2 Combine watermelon in medium bowl with berries and mint.

prep time 10 minutes **serves** 4
nutritional count per serving
0.5g total fat (0g saturated fat);
75 cal; 14.1g carbohydrate;
1.9g protein; 3.2g fiber

watermelon, raspberry, and cranberry salad

14-ounce watermelon, cut
 into ¾-inch pieces
1 cup fresh raspberries
½ cup diet cranberry juice
¼ cup fresh mint leaves

1 Combine ingredients in medium bowl. Refrigerate 15 minutes.

prep time 10 minutes
(+ refrigeration) **serves** 2
nutritional count per serving
0.9g total fat (0.1g saturated fat);
181 cal; 33.6g carbohydrate;
6.7g protein; 5.0g fiber

tip This fruit salad is delicious and loaded with healthy goodness. Blueberries are full of antioxidants and have been shown to lower cholesterol. If you don't have a melon baller, just cut the watermelon into even-sized square chunks.

watermelon and berry salad

tip This refreshing and bright ruby red fruit salad is excellent any time of day, and is great served with a dollop of fruity yogurt on top.

watermelon, raspberry, and cranberry salad

Weeknight standbys

At the end of the day when time is limited, energy is depleted, and stomachs are hungry, these standby meals mean that dinner can be on the table with a minimum amount of fuss.

lemon fish parcels

15-ounce can whole peeled
  baby potatoes, drained,
  halved
12 ounces asparagus, trimmed
4 × 7-ounce firm white fish
  filets
¼ cup lemon juice

prep + cook time 25 minutes
serves 4
nutritional count per serving
4.6g total fat (1.4g saturated fat);
255 cal; 8.4g carbohydrate;
43.6g protein; 1.9g fiber

1 Preheat oven to 400°F/375°F convection.
2 Place four large squares of parchment paper on top of four large squares of foil; layer potato and asparagus on squares. Top with fish filets. Drizzle fish with juice; enclose fish in foil.
3 Place parcels on baking sheet; cook about 15 minutes.

peppered beef steaks

2 beef tenderloin steaks (8
  ounces)
1 tablespoon drained green
  peppercorns
¼ cup heavy cream
⅓ cup beef stock

prep + cook time 25 minutes
serves 2
nutritional count per serving
17.3g total fat (10g saturated fat);
270 cal; 1.6g carbohydrate;
27.4g protein; 0g fiber

1 Cook beef in heated oiled medium frying pan until done as desired. Remove from heat; cover to keep warm.
2 Add peppercorns, cream, and stock to pan; bring to a boil. Reduce heat; simmer, uncovered, until thickened slightly.

tip You can use any firm white fish in this recipe. Snapper and cod are both good choices. Remove any small bones with tweezers.

lemon fish parcels

tip Serve these juicy peppery steaks with roasted baby carrots and steamed or microwaved crunchy broccolini.

peppered beef steaks

tip Julienning is a method of cutting vegetables into long thin strips (also called matchsticks). You can buy "julienne peelers" that have very sharp teeth, or, alternatively, just cut the strips very carefully using a sharp knife.

snapper filets with ginger soy syrup

tip Wok cooking requires neither much fat nor time, making stir-frying one of the quickest ways to get a delicious and healthy dinner on the table.

beef and black bean stir-fry

snapper filets with ginger soy syrup

2 medium carrots, cut into matchsticks

2 medium zucchini, cut into matchsticks

4 × 9-ounce snapper filets, skin on

1 cup bottled sweet chili, ginger, and soy marinade

prep + cook time 35 minutes
serves 4
nutritional count per serving
4.6g total fat (1.7g saturated fat); 312 cal; 5.4g carbohydrate; 60.4g protein; 2.4g fiber

1 Boil, steam, or microwave carrots and zucchini, separately, until tender.
2 Meanwhile, score fish skin. Cook fish, skin-side down, in heated oiled large frying pan about 5 minutes. Turn fish; cook about 3 minutes. Remove from pan.
3 Add ⅓ cup water and marinade to pan; stir until hot.
4 Serve fish with sauce and vegetables.

Serve with steamed jasmine rice.

beef and black bean stir-fry

1½ pounds beef sirloin strips

1 large red pepper, sliced thinly

1 bunch baby choy sum (Chinese cabbage), chopped coarsely

½ cup black bean garlic sauce

prep + cook time 20 minutes
serves 4
nutritional count per serving
18.1g total fat (7.1g saturated fat); 416 cal; 12.2g carbohydrate; 49.7g protein; 1g fiber

1 Heat oiled wok; stir-fry beef, in batches, until just browned.
2 Add pepper to wok; stir-fry 1 minute. Return beef to wok with remaining ingredients and 2 tablespoons water; stir-fry until choy sum wilts.

veal cutlets with mustard cream

8 thin veal cutlets
  (1¼ pounds)
½ cup beef broth
½ cup cream
2 teaspoons wholegrain
  mustard

prep + cook time 20 minutes
serves 4
nutritional count per serving
18.8g total fat (11.3g saturated
fat); 348 cal; 3.6g carbohydrate;
36.3g protein; 0g fiber

1 Cook veal in heated oiled large frying pan, in batches, until cooked as desired. Cover to keep warm.
2 Add broth to same pan; cook, stirring, until reduced by half. Add cream and mustard; simmer, uncovered, about 3 minutes or until sauce thickens slightly. Serve veal with sauce.

Serve with fried potatoes and bacon, or a leafy green salad.

steamed mussels in tomato garlic broth

4 cloves garlic, crushed
14½-ounce can diced
  tomatoes
4 pounds small black mussels
½ cup coarsely chopped fresh
  flat-leaf parsley

prep + cook time 30 minutes
serves 4
nutritional count per serving
2.1g total fat (0.5g saturated fat);
109 cal; 8.2g carbohydrate;
13g protein; 2.1g fiber

1 Cook garlic in oiled large saucepan, stirring, until soft. Add undrained tomatoes and ½ cup water; bring to a boil. Reduce heat; simmer, uncovered, about 5 minutes or until sauce thickens slightly.
2 Meanwhile, scrub mussels; remove beards. Add mussels to pan; simmer, covered, about 5 minutes, shaking pan occasionally, until mussels open (discard any that do not). Remove mussels from pan, divide among serving bowls; cover with foil to keep warm.
3 Bring tomato mixture to a boil; boil, uncovered, about 5 minutes or until thickened slightly. Pour tomato mixture over mussels; garnish with parsley.

veal cutlets with mustard cream

tip Veal cutlets, or escalopes, are large but very thin slices of lean veal. They are tender and quick-cooking, and are often coated with bread crumbs and pan-fried in butter, known as wiener schnitzel.

steamed mussels in tomato garlic broth

tip Mussels should be alive until they reach the pot because they quickly become toxic if they die before cooking. Fresh live mussels will be closed or should close quickly when tapped. If they remain open, you should discard them.

italian-braised sausages with beans

8 thick beef sausages
  (2½ pounds)
2 × 14-ounce cans diced
  tomatoes
7 ounces drained marinated
  antipasto vegetables
14-ounce can cannellini
  beans, rinsed, drained

prep + cook time 30 minutes
serves 4
nutritional count per serving
78.1g total fat (36.9g saturated
fat); 983 cal; 23g carbohydrate;
41.9g protein; 16g fiber

1 Cook sausages in heated oiled large
saucepan until browned. Remove from pan;
cut sausages in half lengthwise.
2 Add undrained tomatoes and ⅓ cup water
to same pan; bring to a boil. Return
sausages to pan with antipasto vegetables;
simmer, covered, 15 minutes.
3 Add beans to pan; simmer, uncovered,
about 10 minutes or until thickened slightly.

*We used sun-dried tomatoes, marinated
artichokes, grilled eggplant, and red peppers for
the antipasto mix; however, any combination of
vegetables can be used.*

char siu pork and veggie stir-fry

1¼ pounds pork filets, sliced
  thinly
14 ounces packaged fresh
  Asian stir-fry vegetables
¼ cup char siu sauce
1 tablespoon light soy sauce

prep + cook time 25 minutes
serves 4
nutritional count per serving
5.5g total fat (1.9g saturated fat);
222 cal; 5.7g carbohydrate;
35.9g protein; 0.1g fiber

1 Heat oiled wok; stir-fry pork, in batches,
until browned and cooked through.
2 Add vegetables to wok; stir-fry until just
tender. Return pork to wok with sauces;
stir-fry until hot.

*Use any combination of prepared Asian stir-fry
vegetables available from supermarkets.*

broccoli and garlic bread crumb spaghetti

12 slices stale white bread
1 pound spaghetti
10 ounces broccoli, cut into florets
2 cloves garlic, crushed

prep + cook time 25 minutes
serves 4
nutritional count per serving
4g total fat (0.7g saturated fat);
642 cal; 121.2g carbohydrate;
24.6g protein; 7.7g fiber

1 Remove and discard crust from bread; process bread until fine.
2 Cook pasta in large saucepan of boiling water until tender; drain.
3 Meanwhile, boil, steam, or microwave broccoli until tender; drain.
4 Cook bread crumbs and garlic in oiled large frying pan until browned lightly and crisp.
5 Combine pasta, broccoli, and bread crumbs in a large bowl.

sweet chili pork with pears

4 × 10-ounce pork loin chops
2 small pears, unpeeled, halved, and cored
1 medium red onion, cut into thin wedges
½ cup sweet chili sauce with ginger

prep + cook time 30 minutes
serves 4
nutritional count per serving
22g total fat (7.3g saturated fat);
432 cal; 19.8g carbohydrate;
36.9g protein; 4.1g fiber

1 Cook pork in heated oiled large frying pan; remove from pan, cover to keep warm.
2 Cook pear halves then onion in same pan until browned. Add sauce and 2 tablespoons water to pan; simmer 2 minutes.
3 Serve pork with pear and onion mixture; drizzle the sauce over chops.

veal with lemon and oregano

2 lemons

2 cloves garlic, sliced thinly

¼ cup fresh oregano leaves

8 × 3½-ounce veal escalopes
(scaloppine)

prep + cook time 20 minutes
serves 4
nutritional count per serving
5g total fat (1.4g saturated fat);
225 cal; 0.9g carbohydrate;
43.3g protein; 1.3g fiber

1 Finely grate rind from one lemon (you
need 1 teaspoon). Juice lemons (you need
²/3 cup).

2 Cook garlic and oregano in heated oiled
large frying pan, stirring, until garlic is
browned lightly and oregano is crisp.
Remove with a slotted spoon; drain on
paper towel.

3 Cook veal in same pan, in batches, until
browned both sides; remove from pan. Add
rind and juice to pan; cook 1 minute.

4 Serve veal with pan juices; sprinkle the
garlic and oregano mixture over it.

We used thin veal scallops in this recipe.

Serve with mixed salad leaves.

chicken and mushrooms in oyster sauce

1¼ pounds chicken breast
filet, sliced thinly

1 pound mixed mushrooms,
chopped coarsely

7 ounces gai lan (Chinese
broccoli), chopped coarsely

⅓ cup oyster sauce

prep + cook time 20 minutes
serves 4
nutritional count per serving
12.8g total fat (3.8g saturated
fat); 298 cal; 6g carbohydrate;
37.1g protein; 5g fiber

1 Heat oiled wok; stir-fry chicken, in
batches, until cooked; remove from wok.

2 Add mushrooms; stir-fry until tender. Add
gai lan, oyster sauce, and 2 tablespoons
water; stir-fry until vegetables are tender.

tip Because veal escalopes are a very lean cut of meat, they dry out quickly if overcooked. Fry them over a high heat for as little time as possible.

veal with lemon
and oregano

tip We used fresh shiitake, oyster, and enoki mushrooms in this recipe, but you can use any combination you like.

chicken and mushrooms in oyster sauce

tip Once you know how to make caramelized fruit, you'll be caramelizing everything from apples and pineapple to peaches and bananas. Serve them with vanilla ice cream.

caramelized pears

tip Serve this light and refreshing dessert with Greek or vanilla yogurt.

fresh peaches with lemon and mint

caramelized pears

4 medium pears
2 tablespoons butter
½ cup firmly packed
   brown sugar
2 tablespoons espresso

prep + cook time 25 minutes
serves 4
nutritional count per serving
8.1g total fat (5.2g saturated fat);
299 cal; 50g carbohydrate;
0.7g protein; 3.2g fiber

1 Peel and core pears; cut each pear into eight wedges.
2 Melt butter in large frying pan, add pears; cook, stirring occasionally, until softened slightly.
3 Sprinkle sugar over pears; reduce heat. Cook, stirring occasionally, until sugar dissolves. Bring to a boil; boil 1 minute. Add espresso; cook, over high heat, about 2 minutes or until mixture is syrupy.
4 Serve pears drizzled with syrup.

Serve with vanilla ice cream.

fresh peaches with lemon and mint

6 medium peaches
¼ cup loosely packed fresh
   baby mint leaves
2 tablespoons lemon juice
1 tablespoon honey

prep time 10 minutes
(+ standing) **serves** 6
nutritional count per serving
0.2g total fat (0g saturated fat);
60 cal; 12.1g carbohydrate;
1.3g protein; 2g fiber

1 Halve and pit peaches; cut into wedges into serving bowl. Sprinkle mint leaves over; drizzle the combined juice and honey over peaches. Stand at room temperature for 20 minutes before serving.

raspberry coconut creams

1¼ cups heavy cream
⅔ cup thick vanilla pudding
3½ ounces coconut
   macaroons, crumbled
15 ounces raspberries

prep + cook time 15 minutes
serves 6
nutritional count per serving
23.8g total fat (15.9g saturated
fat); 298 cal; 17g carbohydrate;
3.2g protein; 3g fiber

1 Whip cream in small bowl with electric mixer until soft peaks form; transfer to medium bowl.
2 Fold in pudding and crumbled macaroons. Layer into serving glasses with raspberries.

apricot crumbles

4 large apricots, halved, pitted
¾ cup natural muesli
   (granola)
1 tablespoon brown sugar
2 tablespoons honey

prep + cook time 25 minutes
serves 4
nutritional count per serving
1.6g total fat (0.4g saturated fat);
147 cal; 29g carbohydrate;
2.3g protein; 3.6g fiber

1 Preheat oven to 400°F/375°F convection.
2 Place apricots, cut-side up, on baking sheet; sprinkle with combined muesli, sugar, honey, and 1 tablespoon water. Bake about 15 minutes or until fruit is tender.

Serve with sweetened ricotta cheese.

watermelon and berry granita

1¾ pounds coarsely chopped
   seedless watermelon
1 pound frozen mixed berries
3 cups ice cubes
¼ cup confectioner's sugar

prep time 15 minutes **serves** 6
nutritional count per serving
0.7g total fat (0.4g saturated fat);
107 cal; 22g carbohydrate;
1.3g protein; 4.2g fiber

1 Blend or process watermelon and berries, in batches, until almost smooth; push batches through sieve into large bowl. Discard solids.
2 Return watermelon mixture to processor; add ice and sugar. Process until ice is crushed.

black forest ice cream sandwiches

14½-ounce can pitted
   black cherries in syrup
¼ cup superfine sugar
7 ounces vanilla ice cream,
   softened
8 large soft sugar cookies

prep + cook time 20 minutes
serves 4
nutritional count per serving
14.9g total fat (11g saturated fat);
483 cal; 78.7g carbohydrate;
6.3g protein; 3.1g fiber

1 Drain cherries; reserve syrup. Stir syrup and sugar in small saucepan over heat until sugar dissolves. Boil, uncovered, about 5 minutes or until syrup thickens slightly. Cool 5 minutes.
2 Sandwich softened ice cream between cookies. Freeze until firm. Place on serving plates; top with cherries then drizzle with syrup.

From the veggie patch

Put these vegetable dishes on the table and watch them vanish. These recipes show how you can quickly and easily get your five servings of veggies a day.

potato, prosciutto, and pomegranate salad

10 medium finger or new
   potatoes (2 pounds), halved
   lengthwise
6 slices prosciutto
3 ounces baby spinach leaves
½ cup pomegranate seeds

prep + cook time 20 minutes
serves 4
nutritional count per serving
1.7g total fat (0.6g saturated fat);
214 cal; 37.1g carbohydrate;
10.6g protein; 4g fiber

1 Cook potatoes in saucepan of boiling water 10 minutes or until just tender; drain. Cool, peel; cut into ⅓-inch pieces.
2 Preheat broiler. Broil prosciutto about 5 minutes or until crisp; chop coarsely.
3 Combine spinach, potato, prosciutto, and seeds in large bowl.

You need to buy a medium pomegranate to get ½ cup seeds. To remove the pulp, cut the pomegranate in half, then hit the back of the fruit with a wooden spoon – the seeds usually fall out easily. Discard the shell and white pith.

beet and feta salad

15-ounce can whole baby
   beets, drained, halved
3½ ounces mesclun (mixed
   greens)
1 cup firmly packed fresh
   mint leaves
8-ounce jar marinated feta
   in oil

prep time 10 minutes **serves** 4
nutritional count per serving
9g total fat (5.8g saturated fat);
151 cal; 7.7g carbohydrate;
8.3g protein; 3.3g fiber

1 Divide combined beets, mesclun, and mint among serving bowls.
2 Drain feta, reserving 2 tablespoons of oil. Chop feta into cubes, divide among serving bowls. Serve salad with reserved oil drizzled over the top.

potato, prosciutto, and pomegranate salad

tip Pomegranate is a dark, leathery-skinned fruit about the size of a large orange. Like passionfruit, once you cut through the tough outer skin, the inside is made up of hundreds of seeds. The pulp has a unique tangy sweet-sour flavor and the seeds give it a good crunch.

beet and feta salad

tip Mesclun is a commercial blend of green salad leaves, including baby spinach leaves, curly endive, and mizuna. It is also sold as salad mix or gourmet salad mix.

spinach, bacon, and poached egg salad

parmesan and baby spinach salad

spinach, bacon, and poached egg salad

4 eggs
8 strips bacon
4 ounces baby spinach leaves
⅓ cup Italian dressing
(*see page 60*)

prep + cook time 20 minutes
serves 4
nutritional count per serving
29.5g total fat (7.8g saturated
fat); 404 cal; 1.6g carbohydrate;
33.9g protein; 0g fiber

1 Half fill a large frying pan with water; bring to a boil. Break eggs into the pan; return water just to a boil. Cover pan, turn off heat; stand about 4 minutes or until a light film of white sets over each yolk. Using a slotted spoon, remove eggs from pan; rest spoon on paper-towel-lined saucer to blot up poaching liquid.
2 Cook bacon in heated oiled large frying pan until crisp; drain on paper towels. Chop coarsely.
3 Combine spinach, dressing, and bacon in large bowl. Serve salad topped with poached eggs.

Instead of making the dressing, buy one from the supermarket, or use your favorite dressing.

parmesan and baby spinach salad

3½ ounces baby spinach
leaves
2 ounces shaved parmesan
cheese
1 tablespoon toasted pine nuts
¼ cup balsamic and garlic
dressing (*see page 60*)

prep time 15 minutes **serves** 4
nutritional count per serving
15.7g total fat (4.1g saturated
fat); 166 cal; 0.6g carbohydrate;
5.9g protein; 0.2g fiber

1 Place spinach, cheese, and nuts in large bowl. Add dressing; toss to combine.

Instead of making the dressing, buy one from the supermarket, or use your favorite dressing.

mixed tomato caprese salad

2 pounds small mixed variety
   tomatoes, sliced thinly
4 bocconcini mozzarella balls
   (8 ounces), sliced thinly
1/3 cup coarsely chopped fresh
   basil
1/4 cup balsamic and garlic
   dressing (*see page 60*)

prep time 20 minutes **serves** 4
nutritional count per serving
19.2g total fat (7.4g saturated
fat); 249 cal; 14.9g carbohydrate;
12.9g protein; 3.1g fiber

1 Layer tomato, cheese, and basil on serving
plate; drizzle balsamic dressing over salad.

*Instead of making the dressing, buy one from the
supermarket, or use your favorite dressing.*

mixed cabbage coleslaw

6 cups (1 pound) shredded
   mixed cabbage
1 medium carrot,
   grated coarsely
4 green onions, sliced thinly
1/3 cup Asian dressing
   (*see page 60*)

prep time 20 minutes **serves** 4
nutritional count per serving
5.7g total fat (1g saturated fat);
89 cal; 4.7g carbohydrate;
2.6g protein; 4.7g fiber

1 Combine cabbage, carrot, and onion in
large bowl. Add dressing; toss to combine.

*Instead of making the dressing, buy one from the
supermarket, or use your favorite dressing.*

tip We used green, black, and vine-ripened tomatoes. For an extra indulgence, use the larger buffalo-milk mozzarella instead of bocconcini.

mixed tomato caprese salad

tip We used green, red, and Napa cabbage in this coleslaw. Elongated in shape with pale green, crinkly leaves, Napa (or Chinese) cabbage is readily available from most supermarkets.

mixed cabbage coleslaw

tip Watercress are deep green, clover-shaped leaves that have a peppery, spicy flavor. They complement the smoky, mild trout and the delicate, creamy texture and rich, sweet taste of the brie. Watercress is highly perishable so it should be used on the day it is bought.

smoked trout, brie, and cranberry salad

tip To trim the woody bottoms of the asparagus, gently bend the asparagus at the base and it will snap at its natural breaking point – where the woody texture turns to crispness.

smoked salmon, egg, and asparagus salad

smoked trout, brie, and cranberry salad

12 ounces trimmed watercress

7 ounces smoked trout, flaked coarsely

4 ounces brie cheese, sliced thinly

⅓ cup cranberry and raspberry vinaigrette (*see page 61*)

1 Divide watercress, trout, and cheese among serving plates; drizzle the vinaigrette over the top.

Instead of making the vinaigrette, buy one from the supermarket, or use your favorite vinaigrette.

prep time 10 minutes **serves** 4
nutritional count per serving
16.5g total fat (6.5g saturated fat); 247 cal; 2.7g carbohydrate; 20.5g protein; 3.7g fiber

smoked salmon, egg, and asparagus salad

12 ounces asparagus, trimmed

7 ounces sliced smoked salmon

4 hard-boiled eggs, quartered

⅓ cup creamy dill dressing (*see page 61*)

1 Cook asparagus on heated oiled grill pan (or grill or barbecue) until tender.
2 Divide salmon, asparagus, and eggs among serving plates; drizzle the dressing over the top.

Instead of making the dressing, buy one from the supermarket, or use your favorite dressing.

prep + cook time 20 minutes
serves 4
nutritional count per serving
13.3 g total fat (5.1g saturated fat); 200 cal; 1.5g carbohydrate; 18.4g protein; 0.9g fiber

summer squash salad

2 pounds mixed patty-pan
  squash, halved
7 ounces baby new potatoes,
  halved
½ cup Italian dressing
  (*see page 60*)
8 ounces cherry tomatoes,
  halved

prep + cook time 30 minutes
serves 4
nutritional count per serving
4.6g total fat (0.6g saturated fat);
70 cal; 4.1g carbohydrate;
2.1g protein; 2.1g fiber

1 Boil, steam, or microwave squash and
potatoes, separately, until tender; drain.
2 Combine warm squash and potatoes with
remaining ingredients in large bowl.

*We used yellow and green patty-pan squash, just
the one variety can be used if you prefer.*

*Instead of making the dressing, buy one from the
supermarket, or use your favorite dressing.*

soba salad with tatsoi and mandarin

6 ounces soba noodles
⅓ cup Asian dressing
  (*see page 60*)
2 medium mandarins,
  segmented, chopped
  coarsely
3½ ounces tatsoi or
  mache leaves

prep + cook time 20 minutes
serves 4
nutritional count per serving
9.4g total fat (2.5g saturated fat);
161 cal; 15.4g carbohydrate;
2.3g protein; 2.8g fiber

1 Cook noodles in medium saucepan of
boiling water, uncovered, until tender;
drain. Rinse under cold water; drain.
2 Place noodles and dressing in large bowl
with remaining ingredients; toss gently.

*Instead of making the dressing, buy one from the
supermarket, or use your favorite dressing.*

*Tatsoi, also known as rosette bok choy, is a
slightly tougher version of bok choy. It was
developed to grow close to the ground so it is
easily protected from frost. Available from good
greengrocers, tatsoi has a very short shelf life,
so use it immediately.*

teriyaki beef and radish salad

¼ cup teriyaki sauce
1-pound piece of beef
   rump steak
4 ounces baby mesclun
   (mixed greens)
2 red radishes, sliced thinly

prep + cook time 25 minutes
serves 4
nutritional count per serving
5.8g total fat (2.5g saturated fat);
171 cal; 0.8g carbohydrate;
28.4g protein; 0.7g fiber

1 Combine teriyaki sauce and beef in
medium bowl; refrigerate 10 minutes. Drain.
2 Cook drained beef on oiled grill pan (or
grill or barbecue) until cooked as desired.
Cover, stand 5 minutes; slice beef thinly.
3 Combine beef, mesclun, and radish in
large bowl.

mixed leaf salad with cranberry and raspberry vinaigrette

7 ounces mixed salad leaves
½ cup sliced almonds, toasted
½ cup dried cranberries
⅓ cup cranberry and
   raspberry vinaigrette
     (*see page 61*)

prep time 15 minutes **serves** 8
nutritional count per serving
5.7g total fat (0.6g saturated fat);
88 cal; 7.7g carbohydrate;
1.3g protein; 1.4g fiber

1 Sprinkle salad leaves with nuts and
cranberries; drizzle the vinaigrette over
to serve.

*Instead of making the vinaigrette, buy one from
the supermarket, or use your favorite vinaigrette.*

turkey, fig, and spinach salad

6 large fresh figs, quartered

3½ ounces baby spinach
  leaves

3½ ounces shaved turkey
  breast, chopped coarsely

¼ cup cranberry and
  raspberry vinaigrette
  (*see page 61*)

1 Place figs, spinach, turkey, and vinaigrette in large bowl; toss gently to combine.

Instead of making the vinaigrette, buy one from the supermarket, or use your favorite vinaigrette.

prep time 10 minutes **serves** 4
nutritional count per serving
3.8g total fat (0.5g saturated fat);
120 cal; 9.9g carbohydrate;
9.6g protein; 3.7g fiber

fennel, macadamia, and feta salad

3 baby fennel bulbs, trimmed

½ cup coarsely chopped
  macadamias, toasted

¼ cup lemon and
  macadamia dressing
  (*see page 63*)

3½-ounce piece feta cheese

1 Slice fennel as thinly as possible (use a V-slicer or mandoline, if you can).
2 Combine fennel, nuts, and dressing in large bowl. Divide salad among serving plates; sprinkle the cheese over to serve.

Instead of making the dressing, buy one from the supermarket, or use your favorite dressing.

prep time 20 minutes **serves** 4
nutritional count per serving
28.6g total fat (7g saturated fat);
297 cal; 3.1g carbohydrate;
6.5g protein; 2.9g fiber

turkey, fig, and spinach salad

tip Turkey breast is exceptionally low in fat and cholesterol, and an excellent source of protein.

fennel, macadamia, and feta salad

tip Macadamias are native to Australia. They have a creamy, crisp texture and a rich, buttery, delicate flavor. They should be stored in the refrigerator because of their high oil content.

balsamic and garlic dressing

¼ cup balsamic vinegar
2 tablespoons lemon juice
2 cloves garlic, crushed
¾ cup olive oil

1 Whisk ingredients in small bowl until smooth.

prep time 10 minutes makes 1¼ cup
nutritional count per tablespoon 10.6g total fat (1.5g saturated fat); 94 cal; 0.1g carbohydrate; 0g protein; 0.1g fiber

italian dressing

⅔ cup olive oil
⅓ cup white wine vinegar
1 clove garlic, crushed
2 tablespoons finely chopped
  mixed fresh herbs

1 Combine ingredients in screw-top jar; shake well.

prep time 5 minutes makes 1 cup
nutritional count per tablespoon
12.2g total fat (1.7g saturated fat); 111 cal; 0.4g carbohydrate; 0.1g protein; 0.2g fiber

We used oregano and basil, use whatever fresh herbs you like.

asian dressing

⅓ cup lime juice
2 fresh long red chilies,
  sliced thinly
2-inch piece fresh ginger,
  cut into matchsticks
¼ cup peanut oil

1 Whisk ingredients in small bowl until smooth.

prep time 10 minutes makes ⅔ cup
nutritional count per tablespoon
6.9g total fat (1.2g saturated fat); 63 cal; 0.3g carbohydrate; 0.1g protein; 0.1g fiber

creamy dill dressing

½ cup sour cream
¼ cup lemon juice
2 tablespoons finely chopped
  fresh dill

1 Whisk sour cream, juice, and 1 tablespoon hot water in small bowl. Stir in dill.

prep time 10 minutes **makes** ¾ cup
nutritional count per tablespoon
3.6g total fat (2.4g saturated fat); 37 cal;
0.7g carbohydrate; 0.5g protein; 0g fiber

blue cheese dressing

⅓ cup buttermilk
3½ ounces blue cheese,
  crumbled
1 tablespoon lemon juice
1 tablespoon finely chopped
  garlic chives

1 Whisk ingredients in small bowl until smooth.

prep time 10 minutes **makes** ⅔ cup
nutritional count per tablespoon
4.3g total fat (2.7g saturated fat); 52.6 cal;
0.7g carbohydrate; 3g protein; 0g fiber

cranberry and raspberry vinaigrette

¼ cup red wine vinegar
½ cup olive oil
¾ cup fresh raspberries
¼ cup wholeberry
  cranberry sauce

1 Blend or process ingredients until smooth. Push through fine sieve into small bowl. Discard solids.

prep time 15 minutes **makes** 1 cup
nutritional count per tablespoon
9.5g total fat (1.3g saturated fat); 100 cal;
3.4g carbohydrate; 0.2g protein; 0.7g fiber

Use raspberry vinegar in place of red wine vinegar for an extra fruity taste. If the dressing is too thick, stir in a little cold water.

tip Macadamia oil has a mild, unobtrusive nutty flavor that works well with seafood salads or other delicate salads that shouldn't be overpowered by olive oil.

lemon and macadamia dressing

tip This classic salad dressing is creamy and sweet with a sharp tang provided by the cider vinegar.

honey mustard dressing

lemon and macadamia dressing

1 lemon
½ cup macadamia oil
⅓ cup finely chopped toasted
    macadamia nuts
1 teaspoon superfine sugar

prep time 10 minutes
makes 1 cup
nutritional count per tablespoon
12.4g total fat (1.8g saturated
fat); 114 cal; 0.6g carbohydrate;
0.3g protein; 0.2g fiber

1 Grate rind from lemon (you need 1
teaspoon); juice lemon (you need ¼ cup).
2 Whisk rind, juice, and remaining
ingredients in small bowl until combined.

honey mustard dressing

½ cup mayonnaise
¼ cup cider vinegar
1 tablespoon honey
2 teaspoons wholegrain
    mustard

prep time 5 minutes **makes** 1 cup
nutritional count per tablespoon
4.1g total fat (0.5g saturated fat);
55 cal; 4.5g carbohydrate;
0.2g protein; 0.1g fiber

1 Whisk ingredients in small bowl until
combined.

broccolini with honey

1½ pounds broccolini, halved
  crosswise
1 tablespoon light soy sauce
2 teaspoons honey
2 teaspoons toasted sesame
  seeds

prep + cook time 10 minutes
serves 4
nutritional count per serving
1.3g total fat (0g saturated fat);
78 cal; 4.1g carbohydrate;
8.8g protein; 7.3g fiber

1 Cook broccolini in large parchment-lined steamer, over large saucepan of simmering water, about 5 minutes or until tender.
2 Meanwhile, combine sauce, honey, and 1 tablespoon boiling water in small bowl.
3 Serve broccolini with the sauce drizzled over; garnish with sesame seeds.

peas with mint butter

2¼ cups fresh shelled peas
3 tablespoons butter, softened
1 tablespoon finely chopped
  fresh mint
1 teaspoon finely grated
  lemon rind

prep + cook time 10 minutes
serves 4
nutritional count per serving
8.6g total fat (5.4g saturated fat);
141 cal; 8.6g carbohydrate;
5.2g protein; 5g fiber

1 Boil, steam, or microwave peas until just tender; drain.
2 Meanwhile, combine remaining ingredients in small bowl.
3 Serve peas topped with butter mixture.

broccolini with honey

tip Broccolini is the product of a naturally occurring romance between broccoli and gai lan – not the result of genetic modification. Choose broccolini with shiny stems and dark green buds and leaves.

peas with mint butter

tip You need approximately 2 pounds of fresh pea pods to get the amount of shelled peas needed for this recipe. You could also use frozen peas.

tip Baby onions, often called pickling onions, are just immature brown onions. They have a delicate sweet flavor and are excellent served with meat or added to salads.

balsamic-glazed baby onions

tip Large, flat portobello mushrooms have a rich earthy, full-bodied flavor and meaty texture, making them perfect for roasting and barbecuing.

roasted mushrooms with ricotta

balsamic-glazed baby onions

1 tablespoon balsamic vinegar
1 tablespoon wholegrain
  mustard
¼ cup honey
1 pound baby onions, halved

prep + cook time 25 minutes
serves 8
nutritional count per serving
0.1g total fat (0g saturated fat);
52 cal; 11.3g carbohydrate;
1g protein; 0.6g fiber

1 Combine vinegar, mustard, and honey in small saucepan; bring to a boil. Simmer, uncovered, about 5 minutes or until glaze thickens.
2 Cook onion in heated oiled large frying pan, brushing constantly with glaze, stirring, until browned and cooked as desired.

roasted mushrooms with ricotta

4 portobello mushrooms,
  stems trimmed
½ cup low-fat ricotta cheese
2 tablespoons coarsely
  chopped fresh flat-leaf
  parsley
2 green onions, chopped
  finely

prep + cook time 15 minutes
serves 2
nutritional count per serving
5.8g total fat (3.4g saturated fat);
120 cal; 2.4g carbohydrate;
12.4g protein; 4.7g fiber

1 Preheat oven to 400°F/375°F convection.
2 Place mushrooms, stem-side up, on baking sheet. Roast, uncovered, about 15 minutes.
3 Meanwhile, combine remaining ingredients in small bowl.
4 Serve mushrooms topped with cheese mixture.

spinach pies

1 lemon

13 ounces baby spinach
leaves

3 sheets frozen puff pastry,
thawed

2 tablespoons pine nuts

prep + cook time 35 minutes
makes 12
nutritional count per serving
11.3g total fat (5.2g saturated
fat); 179 cal; 15.5g carbohydrate;
3.4g protein; 1.5g fiber

1 Preheat oven to 425°F/400°F convection.
Line baking sheet with parchment paper.
2 Grate rind from lemon (you need 1
teaspoon); juice lemon (you need ¼ cup).
3 Cook half the spinach in oiled large
frying pan until wilted. Add remaining
spinach, rind, and juice to pan; cook,
stirring, until liquid has evaporated.
Remove from heat, cool 5 minutes.
4 Using 4-inch round cutter, cut 12 rounds
from pastry. Divide spinach mixture among
rounds. Gather three points of each round
together to form a triangle around filling,
leaving top of filling exposed. Pinch and
twist each corner to secure pasty round.
Place pies on sheet.
5 Sprinkle pine nuts over filling. Bake about
15 minutes or until pastry is browned.

Serve with Greek yogurt.

warm red cabbage and bacon

2 strips bacon, chopped
coarsely

6 cups coarsely shredded
red cabbage

2 tablespoons red wine
vinegar

1 tablespoon brown sugar

prep + cook time 25 minutes
serves 4
nutritional count per serving
3.2g total fat (1.1g saturated fat);
104 cal; 7g carbohydrate; 9.3g
protein; 4.7g fiber

1 Cook bacon in heated oiled large frying
pan until crisp. Drain on paper towels.
2 Cook cabbage in same pan, stirring, about
5 minutes or until softened. Add vinegar
and sugar; cook, stirring, about 10 minutes
or until liquid evaporates.
3 Return bacon to pan; cook, stirring, until
heated through.

fennel and gorgonzola gratins

1¾-pound piece pumpkin, peeled, sliced thinly
2 baby fennel bulbs with fronds
4 ounces gorgonzola cheese, crumbled coarsely
2 cups cream

prep + cook time 35 minutes
serves 4
nutritional count per serving
64.9g total fat (42.7g saturated fat); 699 cal; 16.2g carbohydrate; 12.8g protein; 3.9g fiber

1 Preheat oven to 400°F/375°F convection. Oil four 1-cup shallow pie dishes.
2 Boil, steam, or microwave pumpkin until tender.
3 Slice fennel thinly; chop fronds finely. Layer fennel, half the fronds, three-quarters of the cheese, and the pumpkin in dishes.
4 Heat cream in small saucepan, stirring, until hot; pour into dishes. Cover dishes with foil; bake in oven 20 minutes.
5 Preheat broiler.
6 Remove foil from dishes; broil until browned. Serve gratins sprinkled with remaining fennel fronds.

Fennel fronds are the delicate feathery tips of the fennel plant. They have a light aniseed flavor.

braised baby leeks

16 baby pencil leeks (2½ pounds)
1 lemon
⅔ cup chicken stock
¼ cup flaked parmesan cheese

prep + cook time 35 minutes
serves 4
nutritional count per serving
2.5g total fat (1.1g saturated fat); 92 cal; 8.2g carbohydrate; 6.3g protein; 5.8g fiber

1 Carefully trim root end from leeks, leaving each leek in one piece. Trim leeks into 6-inch lengths; halve lengthwise. Rinse under cold water; drain.
2 Grate rind from lemon (you need 1 teaspoon). Juice lemon (you need 2 tablespoons).
3 Cook leek in oiled large frying pan, 1 minute. Add stock, rind, and juice; bring to a boil. Reduce heat; simmer, covered, 15 minutes or until leek is tender. Uncover; simmer about 5 minutes or until liquid has reduced by half.
4 Serve leeks with cooking liquid drizzled over them and cheese sprinkled on top.

steamed choy sum in oyster sauce

2 pounds choy sum (Chinese
  cabbage), trimmed
1 tablespoon peanut oil
1 tablespoon soy sauce
2 tablespoons oyster sauce

prep + cook time 10 minutes
serves 4
nutritional count per serving
5.2g total fat (0.8g saturated fat);
87cal; 5.2g carbohydrate;
3.4g protein; 3.3g fiber

1 Steam choy sum in bamboo steamer set
over wok of simmering water until just
tender; drain.
2 Heat oil in small saucepan. Add sauces to
pan; cook, stirring, until hot. Serve choy
sum with sauce drizzled over.

lemon and ricotta-filled zucchini flowers

1 lemon
8 ounces ricotta cheese
2 tablespoons finely grated
  parmesan cheese
12 zucchini flowers with
  stems attached (8 ounces)

prep + cook time 35 minutes
serves 4
nutritional count per serving
8.4g total fat (5.2g saturated fat);
118 cal; 1.9g carbohydrate;
8.6g protein; 1g fiber

1 Grate rind from lemon (you need 1
teaspoon); juice lemon (you need 1
tablespoon). Combine cheeses, rind, and
juice in small bowl.
2 Discard stamens from inside zucchini
flowers; fill flowers with cheese mixture,
twist petal tops to enclose filling.
3 Place zucchini flowers, in single layer, in
large bamboo steamer, over large saucepan
of boiling water. Steam, covered, about 15
minutes or until zucchini are tender.

steamed choy sum in oyster sauce

lemon and ricotta-filled zucchini flowers

tip Oyster sauce is a thick, richly flavored brown sauce that is made from oysters and their brine, cooked with salt and soy sauce, and thickened with starches. It goes well with all kinds of meat and seafood, and is often used as an ingredient in a sauce or marinade.

tip Zucchini flowers have a subtle zucchini flavor and are usually stuffed with a mild-flavored filling, and deep-fried, steamed, or oven-baked to make a delicious appetizer. They are available in the summer.

tip Broad beans are also known as fava beans. They are high in fiber and a good source of vitamin C and folate. This recipe is delicious, and would also be excellent with a squeeze of lemon on top.

broad beans and thyme

tip Banana chilies are almost as mild as red peppers but have a distinctively sweet sharpness to their taste. They are found in pale olive green, yellow, and red varieties at most large supermarkets and greengrocers. They are also known as wax chilies or Hungarian peppers.

char-grilled banana chilies

broad beans and thyme

1¼ pounds frozen broad
    beans
2 shallots, chopped finely
5 ounces speck (smoked
    prosciutto), chopped finely
1 tablespoon fresh thyme
    leaves

prep + cook time 35 minutes
serves 4
nutritional count per serving
6g total fat (2.2g saturated fat);
184 cal; 10.2g carbohydrate;
19g protein; 6.4g fiber

1 Drop beans into medium saucepan of
boiling water, return to a boil; drain. When
beans are cool enough to handle, peel away
gray-colored outer shells.
2 Cook shallot and speck in heated oiled
large frying pan, stirring, until speck is
browned lightly. Add beans and thyme;
cook, stirring, until beans are heated
through.

*Speck is cured smoked pork. It is available from
good delicatessens.*

char-grilled banana chilies

4 large red banana chilies
    (1 pound)
1 tablespoon white wine
    vinegar
1 tablespoon olive oil
2 teaspoons finely chopped
    fresh flat-leaf parsley

prep + cook time 30 minutes
serves 4
nutritional count per serving
4.8g total fat (0.6g saturated fat);
57 cal; 2.1g carbohydrate;
0.8g protein; 1.4g fiber

1 Preheat broiler.
2 Cook whole chilies under broiler until
blistered and blackened. Cover chilies with
plastic or paper for 5 minutes; peel away
skin.
3 Arrange whole chilies on serving plates;
combine vinegar, oil, and parsley, and drizzle
it over the peppers.

asparagus with hollandaise

2 tablespoons white wine
   vinegar
2 egg yolks
7 ounces unsalted butter,
   melted
2 pounds asparagus, trimmed

prep + cook time 35 minutes
serves 4
nutritional count per serving
44g total fat (26.9g saturated
fat); 430 cal; 2.8g carbohydrate;
6.1g protein; 2.6g fiber

1 Combine vinegar and 2 tablespoons water
in small saucepan; bring to a boil. Reduce
heat; simmer, uncovered, until liquid is
reduced to 1 tablespoon. Transfer to medium
heatproof bowl; cool 10 minutes.
2 Whisk egg yolks into vinegar mixture. Set
bowl over medium saucepan of simmering
water; do not allow water to touch base of
bowl. Whisk mixture over heat until
thickened. Remove bowl from heat;
gradually whisk in melted butter in a thin,
steady stream, whisking constantly until
sauce is thick and creamy.
3 Boil, steam, or microwave asparagus until
just tender.
4 Place asparagus on a large platter; serve
with hollandaise sauce drizzled over it.

brussels sprouts with cream and almonds

3 tablespoons butter
⅓ cup sliced almonds
2 pounds brussels sprouts,
   trimmed, halved
1¼ cups cream

prep + cook time 15 minutes
serves 4
nutritional count per serving
46.7g total fat (28.4g saturated
fat); 493 cal; 6.6g carbohydrate;
9.5g protein; 7.3g fiber

1 Melt 1 tablespoon of the butter in large
frying pan; cook nuts, stirring, until
browned lightly; remove from pan.
2 Melt remaining butter in same pan; cook
sprouts, stirring, until sprouts are browned
lightly. Add cream; bring to a boil. Reduce
heat; simmer, uncovered, until sprouts are
tender and sauce thickens slightly.
3 Serve sprout mixture topped with nuts.

rosemary potatoes with leek and chorizo

1 pound baby new potatoes, sliced thickly

2 chorizo sausages (12 ounces), cut into 1/3-inch thick slices

1 large leek (1 pound), trimmed, chopped coarsely

2 tablespoons olive oil

1 Preheat oven to 425°F/400°F convection.

2 Combine ingredients in large baking dish. Roast, uncovered, about 30 minutes or until potatoes are browned lightly.

prep + cook time 35 minutes
serves 8
nutritional count per serving
21g total fat (6.7g saturated fat);
289 cal; 10.5g carbohydrate;
12.5g protein; 2.1g fiber

sweet corn with chili coriander butter

4 cobs corn, husk removed

3 tablespoons butter, softened

1 fresh long red chili, chopped finely

2 tablespoons finely chopped fresh coriander

1 Boil, steam, or microwave corn until just tender; drain.

2 Combine butter, chili, and coriander in small bowl. Serve corn topped with butter mixture.

prep + cook time 25 minutes
serves 4
nutritional count per serving
12.7g total fat (6.7g saturated fat); 335 cal; 39.6g carbohydrate;
10.3g protein; 10.9g fiber

celeriac purée

2 cups chicken stock
2 pounds celeriac, trimmed,
    peeled, chopped coarsely
½ cup cream
1 tablespoon finely chopped
    fresh chives

prep + cook time 35 minutes
serves 4
nutritional count per serving
14.4g total fat (9.2g saturated
fat); 195 cal; 7.4g carbohydrate;
5.2g protein; 8.8g fiber

1 Bring stock to a boil in medium saucepan; add celeriac, return to a boil. Reduce heat; simmer, covered, about 30 minutes or until celeriac is tender. Drain.
2 Stand celeriac 10 minutes, then blend or process, in batches, with cream until smooth. Serve garnished with chives.

creamy mashed potatoes

2 pounds russet potatoes,
    chopped coarsely
3 tablespoons butter
¾ cup hot milk

prep + cook time 30 minutes
serves 4
nutritional count per serving
10.2g total fat (6.6g saturated
fat); 246 cal; 30.1g carbohydrate;
6.7g protein; 3.4g fiber

1 Boil, steam, or microwave potatoes until tender; drain.
2 Using the back of a wooden spoon, push potatoes through fine sieve into large bowl. Stir in butter and milk.

celeriac purée

tip Celeriac is a member of the celery family, though it is the root that is used, not the stalks as with celery. It has an earthy and pungent celery-like flavor and a creamy texture. It can be grated and eaten raw in salads, or boiled and mashed or puréed like potatoes.

creamy mashed potatoes

tip The trick to getting smooth, creamy mashed potatoes is to use hot milk instead of cold. For an even more luxurious mash, use heated cream instead of milk.

tip A "polonaise" is the French interpretation of a classic Polish way of presenting cooked vegetables such as broccoli, cauliflower, asparagus, and similar, by topping them with chopped hard-boiled egg, buttered bread crumbs, and chopped parsley.

broccoli polonaise

tip These delicious salty bundles are also fantastic with a squeeze of lemon and a sprinkle of chopped parsley.

prosciutto-wrapped bean bundles

broccoli polonaise

1 stick butter, melted
1 cup stale bread crumbs
4 hard-boiled eggs, chopped
  finely
1½ pounds broccoli

prep + cook time 20 minutes
serves 8
nutritional count per serving
14.3g total fat (8.6g saturated
fat); 191 cal; 6.5g carbohydrate;
7.4g protein; 4.2g fiber

1 Heat half the butter in large frying pan;
cook bread crumbs, stirring, until browned
and crisp. Combine bread crumbs in small
bowl with egg.
2 Boil, steam, or microwave broccoli until
just tender; drain.
3 Top broccoli with polonaise mixture then
drizzle the remaining melted butter over
the top.

prosciutto-wrapped bean bundles

14 ounces mixed yellow and
  green beans, trimmed
8 slices prosciutto
4 tablespoons butter
1 tablespoon rinsed, drained
  baby capers

prep + cook time 30 minutes
serves 8
nutritional count per serving
6.9g total fat (4.3g saturated fat);
83 cal; 1.5g carbohydrate;
3.3g protein; 1.5g fiber

1 Cook beans in medium saucepan of
boiling water until just tender. Rinse under
cold water; drain. Divide beans into eight
equal bundles.
2 Place one slice of prosciutto on board; top
with one bundle of beans. Wrap prosciutto
over beans; continue rolling to enclose
beans tightly. Repeat with remaining
prosciutto and beans.
3 Cook bean bundles in heated oiled large
frying pan until prosciutto is crisp. Remove
from pan; cover to keep warm.
4 Melt butter in same pan; cook capers,
stirring, 1 minute. Serve bean bundles with
caper mixture drizzled over them.

Dinner with friends

Good food and good friends are two of the best things in life, so gather the crew around for some casual eating, a few drinks, and lots of laughs.

crab spaghetti in a bag

13 ounces spaghetti

2 cups jarred tomato
  pasta sauce

10½ ounces cooked crab meat

2 tablespoons finely chopped
  fresh flat-leaf parsley

prep + cook time 35 minutes
serves 6
nutritional count per serving
1.9g total fat (0.3g saturated fat);
345 cal; 62.3g carbohydrate;
16.6g protein; 4.2g fiber

1 Cook pasta in large saucepan of boiling water until almost tender; drain.

2 Preheat oven to 350°F/325°F convection.

3 Combine sauce, crab, parsley, and ½ cup water in large bowl. Add pasta; mix well.

4 Place a double layer of parchment paper (or foil), cut into 12-inch squares, into small bowl; fill with one sixth of the pasta mixture. Gather corners of paper together above pasta mixture to enclose completely; secure with kitchen string to form a bag. Repeat to make a total of six bags.

5 Place bags on baking sheet; bake 15 minutes. Remove string before serving.

asparagus and brie bruschetta

12 ounces asparagus spears,
  trimmed

3 cloves garlic, sliced thinly

1 ciabatta loaf

7 ounces thinly sliced brie
  cheese

prep + cook time 30 minutes
serves 4
nutritional count per serving
16.8g total fat (9.7g saturated fat); 422 cal; 48.5g carbohydrate;
19.1g protein; 3.6g fiber

1 Preheat oven to 400°F/375°F convection.

2 Combine asparagus and garlic in large baking dish; spray with oil-spray. Roast, uncovered, 10 minutes.

3 Meanwhile, cut bread crosswise into 6 pieces; place on baking sheet; heat in oven 5 minutes.

4 Top bread with asparagus mixture and cheese; bake about 10 minutes or until cheese melts. Garnish with lemon thyme sprigs, if you like.

crab spaghetti in a bag

tip Crab meat is available from fish markets and the seafood section of most major supermarkets.

tip Brie has a rich, sweet flavor that varies from buttery to mushroomy, and a heavy, creamy texture. It goes deliciously well with asparagus.

asparagus and brie bruschetta

creamy chickpea and garlic soup

2 × 14-ounce cans chickpeas, rinsed, drained
4 cloves garlic, crushed
2 sprigs fresh rosemary
1¼ cup cream

prep + cook time 30 minutes
serves 4
nutritional count per serving
35.1g total fat (21.9g saturated fat); 435 cal; 18.4g carbohydrate; 9.3g protein; 6.2g fiber

1 Combine chickpeas, garlic, half the rosemary, and 4 cups water in large saucepan; bring to a boil. Reduce heat; simmer, uncovered, 25 minutes or until chickpeas are tender. Remove from heat; cool 5 minutes.

2 Discard rosemary. Using hand-held blender, process soup in pan until smooth. Add cream; stir over medium heat until hot. Serve garnished with rosemary leaves from remaining sprig.

seafood chowder

3 pounds mixed seafood such as mussels, shrimp, and cod
1 small leek, sliced thinly
2 tablespoons all-purpose flour
2½ cups milk

prep + cook time 35 minutes
serves 4
nutritional count per serving
17.2g total fat (7g saturated fat); 623 cal; 16.5g carbohydrate; 98.8g protein; 1.1g fiber

1 Scrub mussels; remove beards. Shell and devein prawns, leaving tails intact.

2 Cook leek in oiled large saucepan until soft. Add flour to pan; cook, stirring 1 minute. Stir in milk and 1 cup water; bring to a boil. Reduce heat; simmer, uncovered, 10 minutes.

3 Add seafood; simmer, uncovered, about 4 minutes or until prawns change color and mussels open (discard any that do not).

We used mussels, uncooked medium king prawns, and white cod filets; you can use any combination of seafood you like.

prawn and miso soup

1¼ pounds uncooked medium
  king prawns
4 individual packets instant
  miso soup
5 ounces baby spinach leaves
1 fresh long red chili, sliced
  thinly

prep + cook time 15 minutes
serves 4
nutritional count per serving
1.9g total fat (0.5g saturated fat);
115 cal; 4.9g carbohydrate;
18.6g protein; 1g fiber

1 Peel and devein prawns, leaving tails
intact.
2 Combine soup packets and 4 cups water
in large saucepan; bring to a boil. Add
prawns; cook until prawns just change
color.
3 Stir in spinach and chili; serve
immediately.

red curry lentils

2 tablespoons red curry paste
2 × 14-ounce cans cooked
  brown lentils, rinsed,
  drained
5 ounces baby spinach leaves
2 tablespoons lime juice

prep + cook time 30 minutes
serves 4
nutritional count per serving
1.6g total fat (0.4g saturated fat);
98 cal; 11g carbohydrate;
7.8g protein; 3.8g fiber

1 Cook curry paste in medium saucepan,
stirring, until fragrant. Add lentils and 1
cup water; bring to a boil. Reduce heat;
simmer, uncovered, about 10 minutes or
until thickened.
2 Add spinach to pan; cook until just
wilted. Remove from heat; stir in juice.
3 Divide curry among serving bowls.

Serve with yogurt.

avocado, bacon, and tomato panini

8 strips bacon

4 panini bread rolls

1 medium avocado, sliced thinly

2 medium tomatoes, sliced thinly

prep + cook time 15 minutes

serves 4

nutritional count per serving
25.8g total fat (6.4g saturated fat); 414 cal; 24g carbohydrate; 20.3g protein; 3.1g fiber

1 Cook bacon in heated oiled large frying pan until crisp.

2 Meanwhile, split and toast cut sides of bread rolls. Fill rolls with avocado, tomato, and bacon.

Use small ciabatta rolls if panini rolls aren't available.

pumpkin and feta bread

7 ounces pumpkin, chopped coarsely

3½ ounces feta cheese, chopped coarsely

½ cup coarsely grated mozzarella cheese

1 ciabatta bread loaf (1 pound)

prep + cook time 35 minutes

serves 8

nutritional count per serving
5.5g total fat (3.1g saturated fat); 185 cal; 26g carbohydrate; 8.3g protein; 2g fiber

1 Preheat oven to 450°F/425°F convection.

2 Boil, steam, or microwave pumpkin until tender; drain, cool.

3 Combine pumpkin and cheeses in medium bowl. Place bread on baking sheet; top with pumpkin mixture. Bake 15 minutes.

Ciabatta bread is also known as slipper bread; it comes in long (about 17-inch) flat loaves as well as individual rolls.

asian broth with prawn dumplings

4 cups chicken stock

⅓ cup light soy sauce

16 prawn dumplings

12 ounces choy sum, trimmed,
  cut into 2-inch lengths

prep + cook time 20 minutes
serves 4
nutritional count per serving
2.2g total fat (0.7g saturated fat);
118 cal; 5.6g carbohydrate;
18g protein; 1.5g fiber

1 Combine stock, sauce, and 4 cups water in large saucepan; bring to a boil. Reduce heat; simmer broth, uncovered, 10 minutes.
2 Place dumplings in large parchment-lined bamboo steamer; cook, covered, over saucepan of simmering broth about 8 minutes or until cooked through.
3 Add choy sum to broth; cook until just wilted. Divide dumplings among serving bowls; top with hot broth.

chili salt and pepper seafood

2 pounds mixed seafood
  such as prawns, squid, and
  scallops

2 teaspoons sea salt

½ teaspoon five-spice powder

2 fresh small red Thai chilies,
  chopped finely

prep + cook time 25 minutes
serves 4
nutritional count per serving
2.9g total fat (0.8g saturated fat);
130 cal; 1g carbohydrate;
24.6g protein; 0g fiber

1 Shell and devein prawns, leaving tails intact. Cut squid down center to open out; score inside in diagonal pattern, then cut into thick strips.
2 Combine seafood, salt, five-spice, and chili in large bowl.
3 Stir-fry seafood in oiled wok over high heat, in batches, until cooked. Serve immediately.

We used uncooked medium king prawns, squid tubes, and scallops; you can use any combination of seafood you like.

tip Baby Asian greens usually consist of herbs, tatsoi, mizuna, and sprouts. They are found pre-packaged in most supermarkets.

Thai chicken burgers

tip Gnocchi are Italian "dumplings" that are most commonly made from potatoes or semolina. They can be found in most supermarkets and Italian grocery stores.

gnocchi formaggio

thai chicken burgers

2 ounces baby Asian greens
1 pound ground chicken
¼ cup Thai chili jam or sauce
4 ciabatta bread rolls,
  split, toasted

prep + cook time 20 minutes
serves 4
nutritional count per serving
14.3g total fat (3.8g saturated
fat); 497 cal; 55.3g carbohydrate;
34.1g protein; 3.5g fiber

1 Chop half the Asian greens finely;
place in medium bowl with chicken and
1 tablespoon of the chili jam. Mix well;
shape into four patties.
2 Cook patties in heated oiled large frying
pan until cooked through.
3 Sandwich patties, remaining greens, and
chili jam between bun halves.

gnocchi formaggio

1 pound potato gnocchi
1 cup cream
2 ounces gorgonzola cheese,
  crumbled coarsely
1 cup coarsely grated pecorino
  cheese

prep + cook time 20 minutes
serves 4
nutritional count per serving
41.7g total fat (27g saturated fat);
612 cal; 38.2g carbohydrate;
20.3g protein; 2.9g fiber

1 Cook gnocchi in large saucepan of boiling
water until gnocchi float to the surface;
drain.
2 Meanwhile, bring cream to a boil in small
saucepan. Reduce heat; simmer, uncovered,
3 minutes or until reduced by half.
3 Remove cream from heat; gradually stir
in cheeses until smooth.
4 Return gnocchi to saucepan with cheese
sauce; stir gently to combine.

*Serve with chopped chives or baby arugula
leaves.*

italian-style lamb cutlets

8 French-trimmed lamb
  cutlets (1¼ pounds)
3½ ounces firm goat's cheese,
  crumbled
¼ cup finely chopped
  sun-dried tomatoes
4 slices prosciutto, halved
  crosswise

prep + cook time 30 minutes
serves 4
nutritional count per serving
11g total fat (5.4g saturated fat);
198 cal; 3.4g carbohydrate;
20.8g protein; 1.3g fiber

1 Cut a small horizontal slit in the side of
each cutlet. Combine cheese and tomatoes
in medium bowl. Press cheese mixture into
lamb pockets.
2 Wrap each cutlet with prosciutto. Cook
cutlets in heated oiled large frying pan until
cooked as you like.

mini lamb roasts

5 ounces roasted red peppers
  in oil
1 cup stale bread crumbs
1½ ounces arugula leaves,
  chopped coarsely
2 × 12-ounce mini lamb
  rump roasts

prep + cook time 35 minutes
serves 4
nutritional count per serving
27.8g total fat (8.6g saturated
fat); 461 cal; 12.6g carbohydrate;
39.8g protein; 0.9g fiber

1 Preheat oven to 400°F/375°F convection.
2 Drain oil from peppers; reserve 2
tablespoons. Chop peppers coarsely.
3 Heat reserved oil in medium frying pan;
cook bread crumbs, stirring, until browned
lightly. Add arugula and peppers; cook,
stirring, until greens wilt. Cool 5 minutes.
4 Cut a horizontal slit in each roast to make
a large pocket, but do not cut all the way
through. Press half the arugula mixture into
each pocket; secure with toothpicks.
5 Heat oiled small metal baking dish over
high heat. Cook lamb, turning, until
browned all over. Transfer dish to oven,
roast lamb, uncovered, about 20 minutes or
until cooked as desired.

Italian-style lamb cutlets

tip These lamb cutlets are packed full of delicious salty flavor. "French-trimmed" means that all the fat and gristle at the narrow end of the bone has been removed.

mini lamb roasts

tip Mini lamb roasts, as they are often sold in supermarkets and butchers, are the rump. If you're after a roast dinner, but don't have the time or energy, a mini lamb roast is the answer.

veal with basil mayo

4 × 6-ounce veal cutlets
1½ cups fresh basil leaves
4 slices prosciutto
½ cup mayonnaise

prep + cook time 30 minutes
serves 4
nutritional count per serving
49.6g total fat (13.4g saturated
fat); 624 cal; 20.7g carbohydrate;
24g protein; 2g fiber

1 Preheat oven to 400°F/375°F convection.
2 Oil a baking sheet. Place cutlets on sheet;
top each with 3 basil leaves and then wrap
in prosciutto (securing with toothpick if
necessary). Roast, uncovered, 20 minutes or
until cutlets are cooked as desired.
3 Meanwhile, blend or process mayonnaise
and remaining basil until smooth.
4 Serve cutlets with mayonnaise.

lemon, pea, and ricotta pasta

2 lemons
13 ounces angel hair pasta
2 cups frozen peas
¾ cup crumbled
  ricotta cheese

prep + cook time 15 minutes
serves 4
nutritional count per serving
6.4g total fat (3.4g saturated fat);
426 cal; 68.9g carbohydrate;
18.9g protein; 6.6g fiber

1 Grate rind from 1 lemon (you need 1
teaspoon). Juice lemons (you need ½ cup).
2 Cook pasta in large saucepan of boiling
water until tender; add peas during last
minute of pasta cooking time. Drain,
reserving ¼ cup cooking liquid. Rinse pasta
and peas under cold water; drain.
3 Combine pasta and peas in large bowl with
reserved cooking liquid, rind, and juice; stir
in cheese.

mediterranean baked fish

4 whole white fish (2.5
pounds) such as small red
snapper
½ cup coarsely chopped
mixed fresh herbs
2 medium lemons,
sliced thinly
4 medium tomatoes, chopped
coarsely

prep + cook time 35 minutes
serves 4
nutritional count per serving
3.5g total fat (1.3g saturated fat);
157 cal; 4g carbohydrate;
25.7g protein; 3.2g fiber

1 Preheat oven to 400°F/375°F convection.
2 Place fish in large ovenproof dish.
Sprinkle herbs into each fish cavity. Spray
fish with oil-spray; cover with lemon slices.
3 Place tomato and ½ cup water around
fish in dish; cook, uncovered, about 25
minutes or until fish is cooked through.

*We used basil, parsley, and oregano; use any
combination of herbs you like.*

prosciutto and sage pork filets

1 pound pork filet
12 fresh sage leaves
8 slices prosciutto
1 tablespoon olive oil

prep + cook time 30 minutes
(+ standing) **serves** 4
nutritional count per serving
8.7g total fat (2.1g saturated fat);
205 cal; 0.1g carbohydrate;
31.5g protein; 0g fiber

1 Preheat oven to 425°F/400°F convection.
2 Cut pork into four equal-sized pieces.
Place three sage leaves over each piece of
pork, then wrap each in two slices of
prosciutto.
3 Heat oil in medium frying pan; cook pork
until browned all over. Place pork on
parchment-lined baking sheet.
4 Roast, in oven, about 10 minutes or until
cooked as desired. Remove from oven; stand
5 minutes. Thickly slice pork.

*Serve with mashed potatoes and steamed
green beans.*

tip Chorizo sausage is a highly seasoned, coarsely-ground pork sausage flavored with garlic, chilli powder and other spices. It's widely used in both Mexican and Spanish cookery. Mexican chorizo is made with fresh pork, while the Spanish version uses smoked pork.

roasted eggplant and chorizo pizza

tip Duck is a lovely rich meat. It's important to cook it skin-side down to get the skin nice and crispy and to prevent the meat from drying out.

duck with caramelized apples

roasted eggplant and chorizo pizza

10 ounces bottled char-grilled
  eggplant in oil, drained,
  chopped coarsely
½ cup seeded kalamata olives
1 cured chorizo sausage,
  sliced thinly
½ cup coarsely grated
  pizza cheese

prep + cook time 25 minutes
serves 4
nutritional count per serving
33.8g total fat (8.6g saturated
fat); 812 cal; 95.3g carbohydrate;
27.9g protein; 6.6g fiber

1 Preheat oven to 425°F. Oil two oven trays.
2 Top pizza bases with eggplant, olives and chorizo, sprinkle with cheese; season. Cook, uncovered, about 15 minutes.

Sprinkle pizzas with fresh oregano leaves, if you like.

duck with caramelized apples

4 duck breasts (1⅓ pounds)
2 medium apples, cut
  into thin wedges
2 tablespoons superfine sugar
1 tablespoon lemon juice

prep + cook time 30 minutes
serves 4
nutritional count per serving
29.2g total fat (8.7g saturated
fat); 457 cal; 16g carbohydrate;
32.5g protein; 1.2g fiber

1 Using a sharp knife, score skin on each duck breast in a ½-inch diamond pattern.
2 Heat large frying pan to very hot. Place duck, skin-side down, in pan; cook about 10 minutes or until skin is golden and crisp. Turn duck over; cook 2 minutes then remove from pan. Stand duck, covered, 10 minutes.
3 Meanwhile, cook apple in same cleaned pan, stirring, 2 minutes. Add sugar and juice; cook, stirring, about 3 minutes or until apple is browned and tender.
4 Slice duck thinly; serve with apple; drizzle any pan juices over the top.

Serve with dressed curly endive leaves garnished with roasted hazelnuts.

balsamic roasted chicken with eggplant purée

8 chicken drumsticks

2 tablespoons balsamic vinegar

2 tablespoons brown sugar

1 large eggplant (1 pound), halved lengthwise

prep + cook time 35 minutes

serves 4

nutritional count per serving

33.1g total fat (10g saturated fat); 554 cal; 9.5g carbohydrate; 53.6g protein; 2.9g fiber

1 Preheat oven to 450°F/425°F convection.

2 Combine chicken, vinegar, and sugar in large shallow baking dish. Cover dish; roast chicken 30 minutes.

3 Meanwhile, pierce eggplant all over with fork; place, cut-side down, on oiled baking sheet. Roast, uncovered, about 15 minutes or until tender. When cool enough to handle, peel eggplant; blend or process eggplant until smooth.

4 Serve chicken with eggplant purée; drizzle any pan juices over the top.

chicken saltimbocca

2 × 8-ounce chicken breast filets

4 fresh sage leaves

4 slices prosciutto

1 cup chicken broth

prep + cook time 20 minutes

serves 4

nutritional count per serving

11g total fat (3.4g saturated fat); 254 cal; 0.2g carbohydrate; 28.5g protein; 0g fiber

1 Cut each chicken breast in half horizontally. Top each chicken piece with sage leaves. Wrap with prosciutto then secure with toothpicks or small skewers.

2 Cook chicken in heated oiled large frying pan until cooked through. Remove from pan.

3 Pour broth into pan; bring to a boil, stirring. Boil until liquid is reduced by half.

4 Serve chicken saltimbocca drizzled with sauce; accompany with lemon wedges.

gorgonzola and sage-stuffed chicken

⅓ cup sun-dried tomatoes
  in oil
4 chicken breast filets (1¾
  pounds)
3½ ounces gorgonzola cheese,
  cut into four even slices
12 fresh sage leaves

prep + cook time 25 minutes
serves 4
nutritional count per serving
20.1g total fat (8.7g saturated
fat); 398 cal; 4.3g carbohydrate;
49.2g protein; 1.8g fiber

1 Drain tomatoes; reserve 2 tablespoons of the oil.
2 Cut horizontal slits into chicken filets, three-quarters of the way through, to make pockets. Divide cheese, sage, and tomatoes among pockets.
3 Cook chicken in heated oiled large frying pan until cooked through. Slice chicken thickly.

lamb racks with mustard maple glaze

4 × 4-chop French-trimmed
  lamb cutlet racks (1½
  pounds)
2 cloves garlic, sliced thinly
⅓ cup maple syrup
2 tablespoons wholegrain
  mustard

prep + cook time 30 minutes
serves 4
nutritional count per serving
15.6g total fat (7.1g saturated
fat); 289 cal; 18.4g carbohydrate;
18.6g protein; 0.5g fiber

1 Preheat oven to 400°F/375°F convection.
2 Using sharp knife, make cuts in lamb; press garlic slices into cuts.
3 Combine syrup and mustard in small bowl. Place lamb in large oiled baking dish; brush with syrup mixture.
4 Roast, uncovered, about 20 minutes or until lamb is cooked as desired.

peach and walnut galettes

1 sheet frozen puff pastry, thawed
¼ cup demarrera sugar
⅓ cup finely chopped walnuts
4 canned peach halves in natural juice, drained

prep + cook time 20 minutes
makes 4
nutritional count per galette
16.4g total fat (5.5g saturated fat); 311 cal; 35.8g carbohydrate; 4.1g protein; 2g fiber

1 Preheat oven to 350°F/325°F convection. Grease baking sheet; line with parchment.
2 Cut pastry into quarters; place quarters on sheet, prick pastry with fork.
3 Divide sugar and nuts among pastry squares, leaving ½-inch border around each.
4 Slice peach halves thinly; divide among pastry squares. Bake about 10 minutes or until pastry is golden brown.

rhubarb soufflé

½ cup superfine sugar
1½ cups coarsely chopped rhubarb
3 egg whites
1 tablespoon confectioner's sugar

prep + cook time 30 minutes
serves 4
nutritional count per serving
1.1g total fat (0.1g saturated fat); 152 cal; 31g carbohydrate; 3.3g protein; 1.3g fiber

1 Preheat oven to 400°F/375°F convection.
2 Grease four 1-cup ovenproof dishes; sprinkle base and sides with 2 tablespoons of the sugar. Stand dishes on baking sheet.
3 Combine rhubarb, 2 tablespoons of the sugar, and 2 tablespoons water in small saucepan. Cook, stirring, over medium heat, about 10 minutes or until mixture thickens. Transfer mixture to medium heatproof bowl.
4 Meanwhile, beat egg whites in small bowl with electric mixer until soft peaks form. Gradually add remaining sugar; beat until firm peaks form.
5 Fold egg-white mixture into warm rhubarb mixture, in two batches. Spoon mixture into dishes. Bake in oven about 12 minutes.
6 Serve soufflés immediately, dusted with sifted confectioner's sugar.

tip Galette is the general French name for a freeform rustic tart, usually consisting of a thin layer of fruit baked on top of a buttery, crisp pastry. Serve this galette warm, straight from the oven, with a healthy dollop of whipped cream.

peach and walnut galettes

tip Rhubarb has thick, celery-like stalks that are the only edible part of the plant – the leaves contain a toxic substance and should be discarded. Although eaten as a fruit, rhubarb is actually a vegetable.

rhubarb soufflé

tip Star anise is the dried star-shaped fruit of a tree native to China. The pods have an astringent aniseed or licorice flavor.

tea-spiced pears

tip Use any fresh melon available such as canteloupe, honeydew, or Crenshaw.

melon and peach tiramisu

tea-spiced pears

1 tablespoon jasmine tea
  leaves
1/3 cup firmly packed
  brown sugar
4 small pears
3 star anise

prep + cook time 35 minutes
serves 4
nutritional count per serving
0.1g total fat (0g saturated fat);
161 cal; 37.5g carbohydrate;
6.4g protein; 2.6g fiber

1 Combine tea leaves, sugar, and 4 cups
boiling water in large heatproof bowl; stir
until sugar dissolves. Stand 10 minutes.
Strain; discard leaves.
2 Meanwhile, peel, halve, and core pears.
Combine pears, strained tea mixture, and
star anise in medium saucepan; bring to a
boil. Reduce heat, simmer, uncovered, about
25 minutes or until pears are tender.
Transfer pears to bowls.
3 Boil syrup, uncovered, until reduced by
half. Serve pears with syrup.

melon and peach tiramisu

1 1/2 cups heavy cream
2 × 7-inch round store-
  bought sponge cakes
1/4 cup peach syrup
1 1/4 pounds chopped mixed
  melon

prep time 25 minutes **serves** 6
nutritional count per serving
22.2g total fat (15.2g saturated
fat); 480 cal; 57.5g carbohydrate;
7.8g protein; 1.8g fiber

1 Beat cream in small bowl with electric
mixer until soft peaks form.
2 Split cakes in half horizontally; trim
brown edges. Using a cutter, cut 12 × 2 1/2
rounds from cakes. Place one cake round in
each of six 1 1/2-cup glasses; drizzle half the
syrup evenly over cake pieces.
3 Divide half the combined melons then
cream over cake. Repeat layering.

crêpes with ice cream and passionfruit sauce

¾ cup cream
½ cup passionfruit pulp
14-ounce packet frozen crêpes
1 quart vanilla ice cream

prep + cook time 10 minutes
serves 4
nutritional count per serving
31.3g total fat (19.3g saturated
fat); 476 cal; 36g carbohydrate;
10.6g protein; 5.3g fiber

1 Warm cream in small saucepan over low heat; remove from heat, stir in passionfruit.
2 Heat crêpes according to directions on the packet. Serve crêpes with sauce and ice cream.

white chocolate and macadamia parcels

4 sheets filo pastry
1 cup soft ricotta cheese
¼ cup coarsely chopped
  roasted unsalted
  macadamias
½ cup coarsely chopped
  white chocolate

prep + cook time 20 minutes
makes 4
nutritional count per parcel
25.3g total fat (12.7g saturated
fat); 407 cal; 34.8g carbohydrate;
10g protein; 0.7g fiber

1 Preheat oven to 350°F/325°F convection. Grease baking sheet; line with parchment.
2 Cut one pastry sheet in half crosswise; spray one half with oil-spray, place unoiled half on top. Repeat process with remaining sheets. You will have four pastry stacks.
3 Center a quarter of the cheese on each pastry stack then sprinkle each with a quarter of the combined nuts and chocolate. Fold ends of pastry towards the center; then roll from one side to enclose filling. Place parcels, seam-side down, on tray.
4 Bake about 10 minutes or until pastry is golden brown. Serve with honey drizzled over, if desired.

crêpes with ice cream and passionfruit sauce

tip If passionfruit is not in season, you can easily buy the pulp in cans from supermarkets.

white chocolate and macadamia parcels

tip There's no limit to the number of variations you could make to these neat little parcels. Instead of white chocolate and macadamias, you could use milk chocolate and pistachios, or dark chocolate and hazelnuts.

tip Strawberries and balsamic vinegar are a food match made in heaven. The rich, sweet and complex flavor of the vinegar brings out the intense sweetness of the strawberries. Topped off with mascarpone cheese, dessert doesn't get much better than this.

balsamic strawberries with mascarpone

tip We used bananas, strawberries, and pears, but try any combination of fruit you like. This recipe makes 1 cup of sauce, which is suitable to freeze.

caramel fondue with fresh fruit

balsamic strawberries with mascarpone

1 pound strawberries, halved
¼ cup superfine sugar
2 tablespoons balsamic
  vinegar
1 cup mascarpone cheese

prep + cook time 5 minutes
(+ refrigeration) **serves** 4
nutritional count per serving
29.8g total fat (20.3g saturated
fat); 376 cal; 21.2g carbohydrate;
5.2g protein; 3g fiber

1 Combine strawberries, sugar, and vinegar in medium bowl, cover; refrigerate 20 minutes.
2 Serve strawberries with mascarpone; drizzle the juices from the bowl over them.

Serve with chopped mint or basil leaves.

caramel fondue with fresh fruit

½ cup firmly packed brown
  sugar
⅔ cup cream
3 tablespoons butter
fresh fruit, to serve

prep + cook time 10 minutes
serves 4
nutritional count per serving
27.7g total fat (18.2g saturated
fat); 479 cal; 52.8g carbohydrate;
3.3g protein; 4.6g fiber

1 Combine sugar, cream, and butter in small saucepan. Cook, stirring, until sugar dissolves and butter melts; bring to a boil. Reduce heat; simmer, uncovered, 3 minutes.
2 Remove from heat; cool 10 minutes before serving with fruit.

We used strawberries, bananas, and pears; you can use any combination of fruit you like.

Hot off the grill

Turn up the heat and start sizzling. Grilling and barbecuing are easy and healthy ways to cook, and versatile too. You can barbecue everything from fish to veggies to steaks.

blood orange and chili-glazed quail

6 quails (2 pounds)
½ cup blood orange juice
1 fresh long red chili, chopped finely
2 tablespoons brown sugar

prep + cook time 35 minutes
serves 8
nutritional count per serving
6.6g total fat (1.7g saturated fat);
123 cal; 4.4g carbohydrate;
11.3g protein; 0.1g fiber

1 Using kitchen scissors, cut along both sides of quails' backbones; discard backbones. Halve each quail along breastbone; cut each in half again to give a total of 24 pieces.
2 Cook quail, covered, on heated oiled grill pan (or grill or barbecue) about 20 minutes or until cooked through.
3 Meanwhile, stir juice, chili, and sugar in small saucepan over low heat, without boiling, until sugar dissolves. Bring to a boil; boil, uncovered, about 5 minutes or until thick and syrupy.
4 Serve quail with syrup drizzled over the top.

grilled steaks with anchovy butter

6 × 8-ounce New York cut steaks
4 tablespoons butter, softened
6 drained anchovy filets, chopped coarsely
2 tablespoons finely chopped fresh flat-leaf parsley

prep + cook time 20 minutes
serves 6
nutritional count per serving
24.3g total fat (12.8g saturated fat); 409 cal; 0.1g carbohydrate;
47.5g protein; 0.1g fiber

1 Cook steaks on heated grill pan (or grill or barbecue) until cooked as desired. Cover steaks; stand 5 minutes.
2 Meanwhile, combine butter, anchovy, and parsley in small bowl.
3 Serve steaks topped with anchovy butter.

Serve with oven-roasted potato wedges and a tossed green salad.

blood orange and chili-glazed quail

grilled steaks with anchovy butter

tip Quail are small, delicately-flavored farmed game birds ranging in weight from 8 ounces to 12 ounces. They are related to the partridge and pheasant.

tip New York cut steak is sometimes called boneless sirloin by butchers. You can make the anchovy butter ahead of time and keep it in the freezer.

tip Sumac is a purple-red spice ground from berries growing on shrubs that flourish wild around the Mediterranean; it has a mild, tart, lemony flavor. It can be found in Mediterranean supermarkets or in spice shops. Try serving these skewers with lemon wedges for an extra zing.

sumac and sesame chicken skewers

tip Entertain with the flavors of Spain and serve tapas to your guests. Bring the colors of the Spanish flag to your table by adding char-grilled red peppers to these delicious smoky, garlicky prawns.

garlic and paprika char-grilled prawns

sumac and sesame chicken skewers

1¼ pounds chicken breast
   filets, cut into ¾-inch cubes
1 tablespoon sumac
1 teaspoon sesame seeds
1 teaspoon black sesame seeds

prep + cook time 30 minutes
makes 16
nutritional count per skewer
2.6g total fat (0.7g saturated fat);
53 cal; 0g carbohydrate;
8.1g protein; 0g fiber

1 Thread chicken onto 16 small bamboo
skewers or strong toothpicks.
2 Combine sumac and seeds in small bowl;
sprinkle sumac mixture all over skewers.
3 Cook skewers on heated oiled grill pan (or
grill or barbecue) until chicken is cooked
through.

*Soak the skewers or toothpicks in cold water for 30
minutes before using to prevent them from
splintering and scorching during cooking.*

garlic and paprika char-grilled prawns

12 uncooked medium king
   prawns
⅓ cup olive oil
2 cloves garlic, crushed
1 teaspoon smoked paprika

prep + cook time 30 minutes
serves 6
nutritional count per serving
12.5g total fat (1.8g saturated
fat); 156 cal; 1.2g carbohydrate;
9.7g protein; 0.5g fiber

1 Shell and devein prawns, leaving tails
intact.
2 Combine prawns, oil, garlic, and paprika
in medium bowl.
3 Cook prawns on heated oiled grill pan (or
grill or barbecue) until they just change
color.

pesto chicken with grilled zucchini

6 medium zucchini, sliced
  thickly lengthwise
1 teaspoon finely grated lemon
  rind
1/3 cup sun-dried tomato pesto
4 × 7-ounce chicken thigh
  filets, cut into thirds

prep + cook time 25 minutes
serves 4
nutritional count per serving
35.1g total fat (10.3g saturated
fat); 484 cal; 4.3g carbohydrate;
36.7g protein; 2.8g fiber

1 Spray zucchini with oil-spray; cook on heated oiled grill pan (or grill or barbecue), in batches, until tender. Place zucchini in medium bowl; sprinkle with rind. Cover to keep warm.
2 Combine pesto and chicken in large bowl. Cook chicken on heated oiled grill pan (or grill or barbecue), brushing occasionally with pesto mixture, until cooked. Serve chicken with zucchini.

Serve with baby arugula leaves or a leafy green salad, if you like.

salmon with creamy dill sauce

4 × 8-ounce salmon filets,
  skin on
1 small brown onion,
  chopped finely
1¼ cups cream
1 tablespoon coarsely chopped
  fresh dill

prep + cook time 25 minutes
serves 4
nutritional count per serving
48.1g total fat (25g saturated
fat); 619 cal; 3.2g carbohydrate;
44.6g protein; 0.3g fiber

1 Cook fish, skin-side down, on heated oiled grill pan (or grill or barbecue) about 5 minutes. Turn fish; cook about 3 minutes. Remove fish from pan; cover to keep warm.
2 Meanwhile, combine onion and cream in small saucepan; simmer, uncovered, 8 minutes, then stir in dill.
3 Serve fish with sauce drizzled over it.

pesto chicken with grilled zucchini

tip Chicken thighs are delicious, but they are often overlooked in favor of the breasts. The thigh is full of flavor and will not dry out as easily as the breast.

salmon with creamy dill sauce

tip Salmon has a wonderfully moist, delicate flavor that is beautifully complemented by this dill sauce. Make sure you get the skin nice and crispy before flipping the filet.

tip Octopus is best cooked just before serving, as it tends to become rubbery when cold. Serve with lemon wedges and a green salad for a light and healthy meal.

barbecued baby octopus

tip Tarragon is known as the "king of herbs" by the French because it is the essential flavoring for many of their classic sauces. It has a mild aniseed flavor and goes very well with many French dishes, but especially egg, seafood, and chicken recipes.

lemon tarragon scallop skewers

barbecued baby octopus

2 pounds baby octopus
⅓ cup lemon juice
⅓ cup olive oil
3 cloves garlic, crushed

prep + cook time 35 minutes
serves 6
nutritional count per serving
13.4g total fat (1.7g saturated
fat); 235 cal; 1g carbohydrate;
27.6g protein; 0.2g fiber

1 Clean octopus, remove eyes and beaks.
Combine octopus with juice, oil, and garlic
in medium bowl. Cover, refrigerate 10
minutes.
2 Drain octopus; discard marinade. Cook
octopus on heated oiled barbecue (or grill or
grill pan) until tender.

lemon tarragon scallop skewers

2 lemons
24 sea scallops without roe
2 teaspoons olive oil
2 teaspoons finely chopped
  fresh tarragon

prep + cook time 15 minutes
makes 8
nutritional count per skewer
1.4g total fat (0.2g saturated fat);
53 cal; 0.9g carbohydrate;
8.9g protein; 0.5g fiber

1 Cut one lemon into eight wedges. Juice
remaining lemon (you need 2 tablespoons).
2 Thread one lemon wedge onto each of
eight bamboo skewers. Thread scallops onto
skewers.
3 Spray heated barbecue grill pan with
oil-spray. Cook skewers about 1 minute
each side or until cooked as desired.
4 Combine juice, oil, and tarragon in small
bowl; serve scallops with dressing drizzled
over.

*Soak the skewers in cold water for 30 minutes
before using to prevent them from splintering
and scorching during cooking.*

grilled haloumi

1 pound haloumi cheese
2 tablespoons lemon juice
1 tablespoon coarsely chopped
   fresh flat-leaf parsley

prep + cook time 10 minutes
serves 6
nutritional count per serving
14.3g total fat (9.2g saturated
fat); 206 cal; 1.7g carbohydrate;
17.8g protein; 0g fiber

1 Cut cheese into ⅓-inch slices. Cook
cheese on heated oiled griddle until
browned both sides.
2 Transfer cheese to serving plate; drizzle
with juice. Serve immediately, sprinkled
with parsley.

pork filet and pancetta kebabs

8 × 6-inch stalks fresh
   rosemary
1¼ pounds pork filet, cut into
   ½-inch pieces
8 thin slices pancetta
   (4 ounces), halved
1 large red pepper,
   cut into 24 pieces

prep + cook time 30 minutes
serves 4
nutritional count per serving
5.3g total fat (1.8g saturated fat);
221 cal; 3.1g carbohydrate;
40g protein; 0.8g fiber

1 Remove leaves from bottom two-thirds of
each rosemary stalk; reserve 2 tablespoons
leaves, chop finely. Sharpen trimmed ends
of stalks to a point.
2 Wrap each piece of pork in one slice of
the pancetta; thread with peppers,
alternately, onto stalks.
3 Spray kebabs with oil-spray; cook on
heated oiled grill pan (or grill or barbecue)
until cooked.

grilled haloumi

pork filet and pancetta kebabs

Salsas

These salsas are great served with grilled chicken, fish, or steaks.

pear, pistachio, parsley, and orange salsa

2 medium pears,
  chopped finely
¼ cup shelled pistachios,
  roasted, chopped finely
¼ cup finely chopped fresh
  flat-leaf parsley
2 tablespoons orange juice

prep time 10 minutes **serves** 4
nutritional count per serving
4.3g total fat (0.5g saturated fat);
120 cal; 16.2g carbohydrate;
2.3g protein; 3.6g fiber

1 Combine ingredients in small bowl.

fennel, yellow tomato, pepper, and lemon salsa

1 large fennel bulb
3½ ounces roasted red
  peppers in oil
7 ounces yellow grape
  tomatoes, quartered
2 tablespoons lemon juice

prep time 10 minutes **serves** 4
nutritional count per serving
1.9g total fat (0.2g saturated fat);
37 cal; 3.1g carbohydrate;
1g protein; 2g fiber

1 Remove fronds from fennel; chop finely (you need 2 tablespoons). Chop fennel finely.
2 Drain peppers reserving 1 tablespoon of the oil. Chop pepper finely.
3 Combine fennel, fronds, peppers, tomatoes, juice, and reserved oil in small bowl.

Fennel fronds are the delicate feathery tips of the fennel plant. They have a light aniseed taste.

pineapple, cucumber, lime, and chili salsa

½ small pineapple
  chopped finely
1 small Lebanese cucumber,
  chopped finely
1 fresh long red chili,
  chopped finely
2 tablespoons lime juice

1 Combine ingredients in small bowl.

prep time 10 minutes **serves** 4
nutritional count per serving
0.2g total fat (0g saturated fat);
54 cal; 10g carbohydrate;
1.5g protein; 3g fiber

peanut, chili, coriander, and lime salsa

½ cup coarsely chopped
  roasted peanuts
2 tablespoons finely chopped
  fresh coriander (cilantro)
1 tablespoon sweet chili sauce
1 tablespoon lime juice

1 Combine ingredients in small bowl.

prep time 10 minutes **serves** 4
nutritional count per serving
9.4g total fat (1.4g saturated fat);
120 cal; 3.9g carbohydrate;
4.7g protein; 1.6g fiber

Coffee break

There is nothing more comforting than the lingering smell of something sweet baking in the oven. And these simple recipes mean that no matter how short on time you are, there can always be a treat ready to have with a cup of coffee or tea.

buttermilk scones

2½ cups self-rising flour
1 tablespoon superfine sugar
2 tablespoons butter
1¼ cups buttermilk

prep + cook time 35 minutes
makes 16
nutritional count per serving
2.2g total fat (1.3g saturated fat);
110 cal; 18.9g carbohydrate;
3.2g protein; 0.9g fiber

1 Preheat oven to 425°F/400°F convection.
Grease deep 7-inch square cake pan.
2 Sift flour and sugar into large bowl; rub in
butter with fingertips. Make a well in center
of flour mixture; add buttermilk. Using a
knife, "cut" the buttermilk through the flour
mixture to mix to a soft, sticky dough.
3 Turn dough onto floured surface; knead
lightly until smooth. Press dough out to ½
inch thickness. Dip 1¾-inch cutter into flour;
cut as many rounds as you can from dough.
Place scones side by side, just touching, in
pan. Gently knead and roll dough scraps; cut
scones from remaining dough.
4 Brush tops with a little water. Bake scones
about 15 minutes.

fruity macaroons

3 egg whites
¾ cup superfine sugar
½ cup desiccated coconut
½ cup finely chopped
  dried apricots

prep + cook time 30 minutes
makes 24
nutritional count per macaroon
1.1g total fat (1g saturated fat);
48 cal; 8.4g carbohydrate;
0.7g protein; 0.5g fiber

1 Preheat oven to 300°F/275°F convection.
Grease baking sheets; line with parchment.
2 Beat egg whites in small bowl with
electric mixer until soft peaks form.
Gradually add sugar, beating until sugar
dissolves. Transfer to large bowl; fold in
coconut and apricots.
3 Drop heaped tablespoons of mixture
about 2 inches apart onto sheets; bake
about 20 minutes. Cool on pans.

tip In spite of its name, buttermilk is actually low in fat. It was originally the name given to the slightly sour liquid left after butter was churned from milk, but today it is made in a similar way to yogurt, by adding specific bacteria cultures to low-fat or non-fat milk. It is easily found in the dairy section of supermarkets.

buttermilk scones

tip These flourless cookies have a wonderfully sweet coconut flavor and are soft and chewy. The apricot adds a delicious fruity flavor, but if you want to try something different, you could replace the apricots with dates.

fruity macaroons

These berry pies are delicious served warm with cream or ice cream and some fresh berries sprinkled on top.

mini berry pies

To give the pastry an extra golden shine, brush it with a little egg before baking.

brown sugar pecan palmiers

mini berry pies

3½ ounces frozen mixed
  berries
1 tablespoon superfine sugar
1 teaspoon cornstarch
2 sheets refrigerated pie
  dough

prep + cook time 35 minutes
makes 12
nutritional count per pie
6.4g total fat (3.4g saturated fat);
118 cal; 13.3g carbohydrate;
1.6g protein; 0.8g fiber

1 Preheat oven to 400°F/375°F convection.
Grease a 12-hole (1-tablespoon) mini
muffin pan.
2 Combine berries and half the sugar in small
pan; stir over heat until sugar dissolves. Bring
to a boil. Blend cornstarch with 1 tablespoon
water; stir into berry mixture. Stir over heat
until mixture boils and thickens.
3 Meanwhile, cut 12 × 2½-inch rounds
from pastry; press into pan holes. Cut 12 ×
1½-inch rounds from remaining pastry.
Divide berry mixture among pastry cases;
top with rounds. Press edges firmly to seal.
Brush tops lightly with water; sprinkle with
remaining sugar. Make small cut in pie tops.
4 Bake about 20 minutes. Stand pies in
pan 10 minutes before turning, top-side up,
onto wire rack. Serve pies warm or cold.

brown sugar pecan palmiers

1 cup pecans
⅓ cup brown sugar
3 tablespoons butter
2 sheets frozen puff pastry,
  thawed

prep + cook time 30 minutes
makes 48
nutritional count per palmier
4.2g total fat (1.5g saturated fat);
57 cal; 4.1g carbohydrate;
0.6g protein; 0.3g fiber

1 Preheat oven to 400°F/375°F convection.
2 Process nuts, sugar, and butter until
mixture is chopped finely.
3 Sprinkle one pastry sheet with half the
nut mixture; fold two opposite sides of
pastry inwards to meet in the center. Flatten
folded edges. Fold each side in half again to
meet in the center; flatten slightly. Fold two
sides in half again to meet in the center.
4 Repeat process with remaining pastry
sheet and nut mixture. Cut pastry into
⅓-inch slices; place, cut-side up, on
parchment-lined baking sheets. Bake about
15 minutes; cool.

vanilla bean butter cookies

1 stick butter, softened
½ cup confectioner's sugar
1 vanilla bean
1¼ cups all-purpose flour

prep + cook time 30 minutes
makes 22
nutritional count per cookie
4.5g total fat (2.9g saturated fat);
68 cal; 6.4g carbohydrate;
0.5g protein; 0.1g fiber

1 Place butter and sifted sugar in small bowl. Split vanilla bean; scrape seeds into bowl. Beat with electric mixer until light and fluffy; stir in sifted flour, in two batches.
2 Knead dough on floured surface until smooth. Shape dough into 10-inch rectangular log. Enclose log in plastic wrap; freeze 10 minutes.
3 Preheat oven to 350°F/325°F convection. Grease baking sheets; line with parchment.
4 Cut log into ⅓-inch slices; place slices about ½ inch apart on pans. Bake about 12 minutes. Cool on pans.

choc-peanut cornflakes

14-ounce can sweetened
   condensed milk
½ cup crunchy peanut butter
3 cups cornflakes
3 ounces chocolate chips,
   melted

prep + cook time 25 minutes
(+ standing) **makes** 25
nutritional count per piece
5.6g total fat (2.3g saturated fat);
138 cal; 17.9g carbohydrate;
3.7g protein; 0.8g fiber

1 Preheat oven to 400°F/375°F convection.
2 Combine condensed milk, peanut butter, and cornflakes in large bowl. Drop level tablespoons of mixture, 2 inches apart, onto two parchment-lined baking sheets. Bake about 12 minutes; cool on sheets before drizzling chocolate over cookies. Stand at room temperature until chocolate sets.

vanilla bean butter cookies

tip These cookies are easy to make and are great for filling the cookie jar. Kids love them, and they also love decorating them. Buy some tubes of decorating icing and let them get their creative juices flowing.

choc-peanut cornflakes

tip For pure crunchy peanut-buttery bliss, you can't do better than these cookies. If you like, replace the chocolate chips with chopped dark chocolate.

coffee almond cookies

1 tablespoon instant coffee
  granules
3 cups ground almonds
1 cup superfine sugar
3 egg whites, beaten lightly

prep + cook time 30 minutes
makes 30
nutritional count per biscuit
6.6g total fat (0.4g saturated fat);
104 cal; 7.9g carbohydrate;
2.8g protein; 1.1g fiber

1 Preheat oven to 350°F/325°F convection. Grease baking sheets; line with parchment.
2 Dissolve coffee in 3 teaspoons hot water in large bowl. Add ground almonds, sugar, and egg whites; stir until mixture forms a firm paste.
3 Roll level tablespoons of mixture into balls; place on sheets 1 inch apart, flatten with hand. Bake about 15 minutes; cool biscuits on sheets.

lemon butter cookies

2 sticks butter, softened
1 cup confectioner's sugar
2 teaspoons finely grated
  lemon rind
2½ cups all-purpose flour

prep + cook time 35 minutes
makes 50
nutritional count per cookie
4.2g total fat (2.7g saturated fat);
76 cal; 8.6g carbohydrate;
0.8g protein; 0.3g fiber

1 Beat butter, sifted sugar, and rind in small bowl with electric mixer until light and fluffy. Transfer to large bowl.
2 Stir sifted flour, in two batches, into butter mixture. Knead dough on lightly floured surface until smooth. Divide dough in half; roll each half into 10-inch log. Enclose in plastic wrap; freeze 10 minutes.
3 Preheat oven to 350°F/325°F convection.
4 Cut rolls into ⅓-inch slices; place on greased baking sheets ½ inch apart. Bake about 10 minutes or until browned lightly. Turn cookies onto wire racks to cool.

mango galettes

1 sheet frozen puff pastry,
  thawed, quartered
2 firm medium mangoes,
  halved, sliced thinly
1 tablespoon brown sugar
1/3 cup shredded coconut,
  toasted

prep + cook time 25 minutes
serves 4
nutritional count per serving
10.8g total fat (6g saturated fat);
270 cal; 37.5g carbohydrate;
4g protein; 3.1g fiber

1 Preheat oven to 400°F/375°F convection. Grease baking sheet; line with parchment.
2 Place pastry squares on baking sheet; prick with fork. Divide mango among pastry squares, leaving 1/2-inch border. Sprinkle sugar over galettes; bake, uncovered, about 15 minutes. Serve galettes with coconut sprinkled over them.

chocolate fig brownies

20-ounce packet brownie mix
4 fresh figs, halved

prep + cook time 35 minutes
serves 4
nutritional count per serving
10.1g total fat (1.8g saturated fat); 217 cal; 28g carbohydrate; 2.8g protein; 1.3g fiber

1 Preheat oven to 400°F/375°F convection. Line 7 1/2-inch × 11 1/2-inch cake pan with parchment.
2 Make brownie mix according to directions on packet. Pour into pan; bake 10 minutes.
3 Place fig halves, cut-side up, over brownie mixture; return to oven, bake 20 minutes. Cool in pan. When cold, cut brownie in eight pieces.

tip This banana tart is delicious and quick to whip up. You could replace the bananas with a number of different seasonal fruits—try strawberries or mixed berries, sliced peaches, nectarines, or apples.

caramel banana tart

tip Use a granola that contains nuts, dried fruit, and coconut for maximum flavor and crunch.

granola bars

caramel banana tart

1 sheet frozen puff pastry,
  thawed
1 tablespoon butter
2 tablespoons brown sugar
2 medium bananas,
  sliced thinly

prep + cook time 30 minutes
serves 16
nutritional count per serving
3.4g total fat (1.9g saturated fat);
71 cal; 8.8g carbohydrate;
0.9g protein; 0.5g fiber

1 Preheat oven to 425°F/400°F convection.
2 Place pastry on oiled baking sheet. Fold edges of pastry over to make ⅓-inch border all the way around pastry. Prick pastry base with fork. Place another baking sheet on top of pastry (this stops the pastry from puffing up during baking); bake 10 minutes. Remove top sheet from pastry.
3 Meanwhile, combine butter and sugar in small saucepan; stir over low heat until smooth. Combine butter mixture and banana in medium bowl.
4 Top tart with banana mixture; bake about 10 minutes.

granola bars

1 stick butter, chopped
  coarsely
½ cup firmly packed
  brown sugar
4 cups natural granola
½ cup self-rising flour

prep + cook time 35 minutes
makes 30
nutritional count per slice
4.4g total fat (2.5g saturated fat);
104 cal; 13.2g carbohydrate;
1.7g protein; 2g fiber

1 Preheat oven to 350°F/325°F convection. Grease 7½-inch × 12-inch pan; line base and long sides with parchment, extending paper 2 inches over sides.
2 Heat butter and sugar in medium saucepan; stir until sugar dissolves. Stir in granola and flour.
3 Press mixture firmly into pan; bake about 20 minutes. Cool in pan before cutting.

Just for kids

Children start developing their eating habits from day one, so get them off to a good start. These recipes will ensure that your kids get the nutrients they need, and will leave you with enough time to take care of other things.

bolognese turnovers

4 sheets refrigerated
  pie dough
4 cups leftover bolognese
  sauce
½ cup finely grated
  parmesan cheese
1 egg, beaten lightly

prep + cook time 30 minutes
makes 16
nutritional count per turnover
14.1g total fat (7.3g saturated
fat); 241 cal; 19.7g carbohydrate;
7.9g protein; 1.3g fiber

1 Preheat oven to 400°F/375°F convection.
Oil baking sheets.
2 Cut sixteen 4½-inch rounds from pastry.
Spoon ¼ cup of bolognese sauce into center
of each round; sprinkle with cheese. Brush
edges with a little egg; fold rounds in half
to enclose filling, pinch edges to seal.
3 Place turnovers on sheets; brush with egg.
Bake about 15 minutes or until browned.

pea and bacon soup

1 medium leek,
  chopped coarsely
1 pound frozen baby peas
1¼ cups cream
2 strips bacon, chopped finely

prep + cook time 20 minutes
serves 4
nutritional count per serving
36.9g total fat (22.8g saturated
fat); 450 cal; 12.3g carbohydrate;
15.3g protein; 8.4g fiber

1 Combine leek, peas, cream, and 2½ cups
water in large saucepan; bring to a boil.
Reduce heat, simmer, uncovered, 10 minutes
or until vegetables are soft.
2 Blend or process mixture, in batches, until
mixture is smooth.
3 Cook bacon in heated large frying pan
until crisp. Sprinkle bacon over the soup.

bolognese turnovers

tip These full-of-flavor snacks are a clever way to use up leftover bolognese sauce. If they're straight out of the oven, the filling is likely to be very hot, as the pastry will trap the steam and heat inside. Let them cool before putting them within reach of the kids, and warn them to be careful when biting into them.

pea and bacon soup

tip The salty, crisp bacon is a lovely interruption to the smooth creaminess of this flavorful soup, and a fun addition for the kids to sprinkle into their own bowls.

tip Instant mashed potatoes, also called dried mashed potatoes or instant potato powder, is a dry, mashed potato mix that is reconstituted with boiling liquid to give light buttery-flavored mashed potatoes. It is available from most supermarkets.

salmon cakes

tip These finger-licking-good chicken drumettes will be loved as much by adults as by the kids. A drumette is just the first section of the wing, which has had the tip removed. They are also sold as wingettes.

sticky chicken drumettes

salmon cakes

2 cups instant mashed
  potatoes (*see tip*)
14½-ounce can red salmon,
  drained, flaked
½ cup finely grated
  parmesan cheese
¼ cup vegetable oil

prep + cook time 30 minutes
serves 4
nutritional count per serving
28.2g total fat (7.2g saturated
fat); 372 cal; 6.4g carbohydrate;
23.4g protein; 0.7g fiber

1 Combine instant potatoes and 2 cups boiling water in large heatproof bowl.
2 Add salmon and cheese to potato mixture; shape into eight patties. Place patties on sheet; refrigerate 10 minutes.
3 Heat oil in large frying pan; cook patties, in batches, until browned lightly and heated through.

Serve with a tomato and herb salad.

sticky chicken drumettes

¾ cup tomato sauce
⅓ cup plum sauce
2 tablespoons Worcestershire
  sauce
16 chicken drumettes
  (2 pounds)

prep + cook time 35 minutes
serves 4
nutritional count per serving
12.4g total fat (3.7g saturated
fat); 329 cal; 28.1g carbohydrate;
25.4g protein; 1.1g fiber

1 Preheat oven to 400°F/375°F convection.
2 Combine sauces in large bowl; add chicken, toss to combine.
3 Place chicken on oiled wire rack over large baking dish. Roast chicken about 30 minutes or until cooked through, brushing with marinade every 10 minutes.

polenta crumbed fish fingers

1¼ pounds white fish filets
1 cup polenta
2 tablespoons finely chopped
   fresh flat-leaf parsley
2 egg whites

prep + cook time 30 minutes
serves 4
nutritional count per serving
5.7g total fat (1g saturated fat);
174 cal; 13.5g carbohydrate;
16.5g protein; 0.6g fiber

1 Cut fish into ½-inch strips. Combine polenta and parsley in shallow medium bowl. Whisk egg whites lightly in another shallow medium bowl. Dip fish in egg white, then coat in polenta mixture.
2 Shallow-fry fish in heated oiled large frying pan, in batches, until cooked through.

You can use any firm white fish filet, such as perch or tilapia, for this recipe.

sesame-crusted chicken and fries

1½-pound package frozen
   potato fries
4 × 7-ounce chicken breast
   filets
1 egg, beaten lightly
½ cup sesame seeds

prep + cook time 35 minutes
serves 4
nutritional count per serving
21.5g total fat (4.7g saturated fat); 553 cal; 36.2g carbohydrate; 50.3g protein; 6g fiber

1 Preheat oven to 425°F/400°F convection.
2 Place fries, in single layer, on oiled baking sheet; bake about 30 minutes or until crisp.
3 Meanwhile, dip chicken in egg, then in sesame to coat. Place chicken on oiled wire rack over large baking dish; bake, uncovered, alongside fries, about 20 minutes or until chicken is cooked through.
4 Slice chicken thickly; serve with fries.

Serve with a dipping sauce made by mixing ¼ cup whole-egg mayonnaise with 2 tablespoons sweet chili sauce.

chicken sausage rolls

12 thick chicken sausages
  (3 pounds)
2 sheets frozen puff pastry,
  thawed
2/3 cup bottled tomato chutney
  or mild salsa
1 egg, lightly beaten

prep + cook time 35 minutes
makes 12
nutritional count per serving
35.1g total fat (13g saturated
fat); 469 cal; 20.5g carbohydrate;
16.7g protein; 4g fiber

1 Preheat oven to 400°F/375°F convection.
Line baking sheet with parchment.
2 Cook sausages in heated oiled large frying
pan 5 minutes or until browned all over.
Cool.
3 Meanwhile, cut each pastry sheet in half;
cut each half crosswise into three rectangles
to make 12 pastry rectangles.
4 Top each pastry rectangle with a sausage;
dollop chutney on sausages. Roll pastry to
enclose sausages, leaving ends exposed.
Place on sheet; brush pastry with egg. Bake
20 minutes or until browned lightly.

peanut butter and alfalfa sandwich

2 slices whole wheat bread
1 tablespoon smooth
  peanut butter
1/4 cup alfalfa sprouts
1 teaspoon sunflower seed
  kernels.

prep time 5 minutes **makes** 1
nutritional count per sandwich
15.9g total fat (2.5g saturated
fat); 286 cal; 44.4g carbohydrate;
5.4g protein; 3.6g fiber

1 Spread both bread slices with peanut
butter. Sandwich sprouts and sunflower
seeds between bread slices. Remove and
discard crust; cut sandwich into triangles
to serve.

*Peanuts can cause allergic reactions in some
children; they are not recommended for children
under one year old.*

tip These "bombs" are far more likely to make you friends than enemies. You could experiment with vanilla or other flavors of ice cream as well.

choc-peanut bombs

tip These pretty little sticks make beautiful gifts – but they should be made on the day you give them. Wrap a pretty fabric ribbon around a bunch of the sticks and your Christmas or birthday present dilemma is solved.

chocolate twists

choc-peanut bombs

1 quart chocolate ice cream,
  softened
¼ cup coarsely chopped
  unsalted peanuts
2 Snickers bars,
  chopped finely

prep time 5 minutes (+ freezing)
serves 4
nutritional count per serving
25.6g total fat (13.7g saturated
fat); 442 cal; 42.6g carbohydrate;
9.1g protein; 2.8g fiber

1 Place ice cream in large bowl; fold in
peanuts and chopped candy bar.
2 Cover; freeze 20 minutes before serving.

chocolate twists

1 sheet frozen puff pastry,
  thawed
2 tablespoons apple juice
3½ ounces milk chocolate
  chips, melted

prep + cook time 25 minutes
makes 24
nutritional count per serving
2.9g total fat (1.7g saturated fat);
49 cal; 5g carbohydrate;
0.6g protein; 0.1g fiber

1 Preheat oven to 400°F/375°F convection.
Line baking sheet with parchment paper.
2 Cut pastry in half; cut each half crosswise
into ½-inch strips.
3 Place juice in small bowl. Dip pastry
strips into juice, one at a time; twist each
strip then place, in single layer, on sheet.
Bake about 10 minutes or until pastry is
golden brown.
4 Dip one end of each pastry twist into
melted chocolate, place on cooled sheet
to set.

strawberry shortcakes

2 sheets refrigerated pie crust

⅓ cup strawberry jam

8 ounces strawberries, quartered

¾ cup heavy cream, whipped

prep + cook time 25 minutes
serves 4
nutritional count per serving
31.4g total fat (17.6g saturated fat); 545 cal; 57.4g carbohydrate; 6.9 protein; 3.3g fiber

1 Preheat oven to 400°F/375°F convection. Line baking sheets with parchment.
2 Using a 3-inch round fluted cutter, cut 12 rounds from pastry; place on sheets. Bake rounds about 10 minutes or until crisp; cool.
3 Spread jam over eight pastry rounds; place four on serving plates. Top shortcakes with half the strawberries and cream, then another shortcake; repeat with remaining strawberries and cream, then top with remaining shortcake.

blackberry ice cream sandwiches

2 cups frozen blackberries, thawed

1 pint ice cream, softened

12 large ginger snap cookies

prep time 35 minutes (+ freezing)
serves 4
nutritional count per serving
14.7g total fat (9.4g saturated fat); 308 cal; 36.7g carbohydrate; 5.2g protein; 6.2g fiber

1 Fold drained berries into ice cream.
2 Working quickly, place half the ginger snaps on parchment-lined tray; place a scoop of ice cream on top of each cookie, then top with remaining cookies. Press down gently. Freeze 20 minutes before serving.

tip These pretty shortcake stacks look beautiful dusted with a little confectioner's sugar.

strawberry shortcakes

tip You can make these little ice cream sandwiches several days in advance, if you like. Instead of the blackberries, use other frozen berries such as raspberries or strawberries, or use a combination of all three.

blackberry ice cream sandwiches

tip Berries are not only delicious but they are also mega-healthy. They are loaded with antioxidants and contain a host of essential vitamins.

berry delicious

tip We used canteloupe, honeydew, and watermelon. If you don't have a melon baller, just cut the melons into pieces with a knife.

minted melon salad

berry delicious

1 pound frozen mixed berries
¼ cup superfine sugar
1 vanilla bean
⅔ cup Greek-style yogurt

prep + cook time 10 minutes
(+ refrigeration) **serves 8**
nutritional count per serving
2g total fat (1.4g saturated fat);
92 cal; 15.5g carbohydrate;
2g protein; 2.6g fiber

1 Combine berries and sugar in medium saucepan. Split vanilla bean, scrape seeds into berry mixture; add bean to pan. Cook over medium heat about 3 minutes, stirring occasionally, or until berries begin to soften. Cool.
2 Transfer berry mixture to container, cover; refrigerate overnight.
3 Discard vanilla bean; serve berries with yogurt.

minted melon salad

5 pounds mixed melons
¼ cup loosely packed fresh
   mint leaves
½ cup apple juice

prep time 20 minutes **serves 8**
nutritional count per serving
0.8g total fat (0g saturated fat);
92 cal; 18g carbohydrate;
1.8g protein; 2.6g fiber

1 Discard seeds from melons. Using melon baller, cut balls of melon into large bowl. Stir in mint and juice.

glossary

ARTICHOKE
hearts tender center of the globe artichoke; purchased in brine, canned, or in glass jars.
Jerusalem a tuber of a species of sunflower, is also known as a sunchoke. Its creamy flesh has a delicious nutty taste and a crisp and crunchy texture.

ARUGULA also known as rocket, rugula, and rucola; a peppery-tasting green leaf. Baby leaves (wild arugula) are both smaller and less peppery.

ASIAN GREENS, BABY usually consist of herbs, tatsoi, mizuna, and sprouts and are found pre-packaged in most supermarkets.

BABA GHANOUSH a roasted eggplant spread or dip. Delicious served with pita bread or vegetables, alongside hummus or on its own.

BACON made from pork belly, cured and smoked.

BASIL an aromatic herb; there are many types, but the most commonly used is sweet, or common, basil.

BEANS
broad also known as windsor, fava, and horse beans; fresh and frozen beans should be peeled twice, discarding the outer long green pod and the beige-green tough inner shell.
cannellini a small white bean that is similar to great northern, haricot, or navy beans, each of which can be substituted for each other.
green also known as French or string beans; this long thin fresh bean is consumed in its entirety once cooked.
kidney medium-sized red bean, slightly floury in texture yet sweet in flavor.
sprouts also known as bean shoots; tender new growths of beans and seeds germinated for consumption as sprouts.
yellow green beans without the chlorophyll; as a result they taste less "green" and are slightly less flavorful.

BEEF
filet a generic name given to a steak cut from the tenderloin.
New York cut boneless striploin beef steak.
rib-eye cut from the muscle running behind the shoulder along the spine. Also known as cube roll; cuts include standing rib roast and rib-eye steak.

tenderloin filet a fine textured, expensive, and extremely tender cut of meat.
BEET also known as red beets; firm, round root vegetable.

BREADS
ciabatta also known as slipper bread; comes in long (about 17 inches) flat loaves as well as individual rounds. Made from wheat flour.
French bread has been formed into a long, narrow cylindrical loaf with a crisp brown crust and a light chewy interior. Is also known as a French stick, French loaf or baguette.
fruit loaf usually containing raisins and other dried fruits and spices.
muffins in this book muffins mean "English muffin"; a round bread made from yeast, flour, milk, semolina, and salt. Pre-baked and sold packaged in supermarkets; split open and toast before eating.
panini roll any white roll used to make a toasted sandwich.
pita also known as Lebanese bread. This wheat-flour pocket bread is sold in large, flat pieces that

146

separate into two thin rounds. Also available in small thick pieces called pocket pita.

rye bread made from 100% rye flour.

BROCCOLINI a cross between broccoli and chinese kale; milder and sweeter than broccoli. Each long stem is topped by a loose floret that closely resembles broccoli; broccolini is completely edible from floret to stem.

BUTTER use salted or unsalted (sweet) butter; 4 ounces is equal to one stick of butter.

unsalted or "sweet" butter, simply has no added salt. You can use regular butter in most cakes and baking, but it's best to stick to unsalted butter when it's called for in a recipe.

CAPERBERRIES a fruit formed after caper buds have flowered; caperberries are pickled, usually with the stalks intact.

CARDAMOM can be purchased in pod, seed, or ground form. Has a distinctive aromatic, sweetly rich flavor and is one of the world's most expensive spices.

CELERIAC tuberous root with a brown skin, white flesh, and a celery-like flavor. Its soft, velvety flesh has the creaminess of potato when mashed, with a subtle celery flavor.

CHEESES
blue mold-treated cheeses mottled with blue veining. Varieties include firm and crumbly stilton types to mild, creamy brie-like cheeses.

bocconcini from the diminutive of boccone meaning "mouthful", is the term used for a round, semi-soft, white cheese.

cheddar, smoked creamy in color and smoky in flavor; available from supermarkets and speciality cheese stores.

cream commonly known as Philadelphia or Philly, a soft cow's-milk cheese.

cottage fresh, white, unripened curd cheese with a grainy texture.

goat's made from goat's milk, has a strong, earthy taste, and is available in both soft and firm textures, in various shapes and sizes, sometimes rolled in ash or herbs.

haloumi a firm, cream-colored sheep's-milk cheese; somewhat like a minty,

salty feta in flavor. Haloumi can be grilled or fried, briefly, without breaking down. Should be eaten while still warm as it becomes tough and rubbery when cool.

mascarpone a fresh, unripened, smooth, triple cream cheese, whitish to creamy yellow in color, with a rich, sweet, slightly acidic taste.

pecorino the generic Italian name for cheeses made from sheep's milk. It's a hard, white to pale yellow cheese. If you can't find it, use parmesan.

pizza a blend of grated cheddar, mozzarella, and parmesan.

CHERVIL also known as cicily; a herb with a mild fennel flavor and curly leaves.

CHICKEN
drumstick leg with skin and bone intact.

drumette small fleshy part of the wing between shoulder and elbow, trimmed to resemble a drumstick.

tenderloin thin strip of meat lying just under the breast, especially good for stir-frying.

CHICKPEAS also called channa, garbanzos, or

hummus; a round, sandy-colored legume.

CHILI available in many types and sizes. Use rubber gloves to seed and chop fresh chilies because they can burn your skin. Remove the seeds and membranes to reduce the heat level.
banana also known as wax chilies or Hungarian peppers, are almost as mild as bell peppers but have a distinctively sweet sharpness to their taste. Sold at greengrocers.
flakes deep-red dehydrated fine slices and whole seeds.
jam a sweet, sourish tangy jam sold in jars at supermarkets or Asian food stores.
long red available both fresh and dried; a generic term used for any moderately hot, long (about 2 inches–3 inches), thin chili.
powder made from dried ground Thai chilies, hotter than fresh chilies.
red Thai small, hot, and bright red in color.

CHIVES related to onions and leeks; has a subtle onion flavor.

CHOCOLATE
dark made of a high percentage of cocoa liquor and cocoa butter, and a

little added sugar.
milk the most popular eating chocolate, mild and very sweet; similar in make-up to dark–the difference is the addition of milk solids.
white contains no cocoa solids but derives its sweet flavor from cocoa butter. Sensitive to heat, so watch carefully if melting.

CHORIZO a sausage of Spanish origin, made of coarsely ground pork and highly seasoned with garlic and chilies.

CHOY SUM also known as pakaukeo or flowering cabbage, a member of the bok choy family; has long stems, light green leaves, and yellow flowers. Is eaten stems and all.

CINNAMON dried inner bark of the shoots of the cinnamon tree; available in stick (quill) or ground form.

CORIANDER also known as pak chee, cilantro, or Chinese parsley; bright-green leafy herb with a pungent flavor. Both the stems and roots of coriander are also used; wash well before using. Available ground or as seeds; these should not be substituted for fresh

coriander because the tastes are completely different.

CORNSTARCH also known as cornflour; used as a thickening agent. Made from corn.

CRAB MEAT is available from fish markets and the seafood section of major supermarkets.
blue swimmer also known as sand crab, blue manna crab, bluey, or sandy. Substitute with lobster.

CREAM
heavy a whipping cream containing a thickener and a fat content of 35%.
sour a thick commercially-cultured soured cream with a fat content of 35%.

CUCUMBER
English also known as the European or burpless cucumber; long and slender with shallow ridges running down the length of its thin dark-green skin.
Lebanese short, slender, and thin-skinned. Probably the most popular variety because of its tender, edible skin, tiny, yielding seeds, and sweet, fresh, and flavorful taste.

CUMIN also known as zeera or comino; has a spicy, nutty flavor.

CURRY PASTES some recipes in this book call for commercially prepared pastes of varying strengths and flavors. Use whichever one you feel suits your spice-level tolerance best.
red a popular curry paste; a medium-hot blend of chili, garlic, onion, lemon grass, spices, galangal, and salt.
rogan josh a paste of medium heat from the Kashmir region of India. Made from fresh chilies or paprika, tomato, and spices, especially cardamom. It may have beet added to make it a dark red color.

EGGPLANT a purple-skinned vegetable.

FIRM WHITE FISH FILET blue eye, bream, flathead, swordfish, ling, whiting, jewfish, snapper, or sea perch are all good choices. Check for small pieces of bone and remove them with tweezers.

FIVE-SPICE POWDER (Chinese five-spice); a mix of ground cinnamon, cloves, star anise, sichuan pepper, and fennel seeds.

FLOUR
all-purpose flour made from wheat.
self-rising plain flour combined with baking powder in the proportion of 1 cup flour to 2 teaspoons baking powder.

GAI LAN also known as Chinese broccoli, gai larn, kanah, gai lum, and Chinese kale; stems are used more than its coarse leaves.

GINGER also known as green or root ginger; the thick root of a tropical plant.
pickled pink available packaged from Asian grocery stores; pickled paper-thin shavings of ginger in a mixture of vinegar, sugar, and natural coloring.

GOLDEN SYRUP a by-product of refined sugarcane; pure maple syrup or honey can be substituted.

HARISSA a Moroccan sauce or paste made from dried chilies, cumin, garlic, oil, and caraway seeds. Available in supermarkets and Middle-Eastern food shops.

HORSERADISH CREAM a paste of grated horseradish, mustard seed, oil, and sugar.

LEEK a member of the onion family; looks like a giant green onion but is more subtle and mild in flavor.
baby or pencil leeks are young, slender leeks that can be cooked and eaten like asparagus.

LEMON GRASS a tall, clumping, lemon-smelling and -tasting, sharp-edged grass; the white part of the stem is chopped and used in Asian cooking.

LEMON PEPPER SEASONING a blend of crushed black pepper, lemon, herbs, and spices.

LENTILS (red, brown, yellow) dried pulses often identified by and named after their color.

MAPLE SYRUP a thin syrup distilled from the sap of the maple tree. Maple-flavored syrup or pancake syrup is not an adequate substitute for the real thing.

MESCLUN a salad mix of young lettuce and other green leaves, including baby spinach leaves, mizuna, and curly endive.

MISO Japan's famous bean paste made from fermented soy beans. It varies in color, texture, and saltiness and is used for flavoring soups.

MOROCCAN SEASONING is available from most Middle-Eastern food stores, spice shops, and major supermarkets. A blend of turmeric, cinnamon, and cumin.

MUSTARD
powder finely ground white (yellow) mustard seeds.
wholegrain also known as seeded. A French-style coarse-grain mustard made from crushed mustard seeds and dijon-style French mustard.

NOODLES
soba a thin spaghetti-like pale brown noodle from Japan made from buckwheat and varying proportions of wheat flour.

OLIVES
green those harvested before fully ripened and are, as a rule, denser and more bitter than their black relatives.
kalamata small, sharp-tasting, brine-cured black olives.
Sicilian dark olive-green in color; smooth and fine-skinned with a crisp and crunchy bite, and a piquant, buttery flavor.

ONIONS
baby or pickling onions are also known as cocktail onions; they are just baby brown onions but are larger than shallots.
green also known as scallion; an immature onion picked before the bulb has formed, it has a long, bright-green edible stalk.
red also known as Spanish, red Spanish, or Bermuda onion; a sweet-flavored, large onion, purple-red in color.
shallots or French shallots, golden shallots, or eschalots; small, brown-skinned, elongated members of the onion family.

PANCETTA cured pork belly; bacon can be substituted.

PAPRIKA ground dried sweet bell pepper; there are many types available including sweet, hot, mild, and smoked.

PARSLEY, FLAT-LEAF also known as continental parsley or Italian parsley.

PATTY-PAN SQUASH also known as crookneck or custard marrow pumpkins; a round, slightly flat summer squash yellow to pale-green in color with a scalloped edge.

PEPPER also known as bell pepper or, simply, pepper. Comes in many colors: green, yellow, red, orange, and purplish-black. Discard seeds and membranes before use.
roasted available loose from delis or packed in jars in oil or brine.

POLENTA (cornmeal) a flour-like meal made of dried corn sold ground in several different textures; also the name of the dish made from it.

POMEGRANATE a reddish fruit about the size of an orange. The individual cells contain seed kernels that are surrounded by an edible juice-filled sac (pulp).

POTATOES
baby new not a separate variety but an early harvest with very thin skin; can be used unpeeled.
finger small, finger-shaped potato with a nutty flavor.
Yukon large, floury, and yellow fleshed; great mashed and fried.

PRAWNS also known as shrimp.

PRESERVED LEMON RIND a North African specialty; lemons are quartered and preserved in salt and lemon juice or water. To use, remove and discard pulp, squeeze juice from rind, rinse rind well; slice thinly. Available from delicatessens and most major supermarkets.

PROSCIUTTO cured, air-dried, pressed ham.

RADICCHIO a member of the chicory family. Has dark burgundy leaves and a strong bitter flavor.

RAISINS dried sweet grapes.

RHUBARB has thick, celery-like stalks that can reach up to 2 feet long; the stalks are the only edible portion of the plant—the leaves contain a toxic substance.

ROSEWATER an extract made from crushed rose petals; called gulab in India. Don't confuse with rose essence, which is more concentrated. Available from health-food stores.

SAUCES
barbecue a spicy, tomato-based sauce used as a condiment.
black bean a Chinese sauce made from fermented soy beans, spices, water, and wheat flour.
char siu a Chinese barbecue sauce made from sugar, water, salt, fermented soy bean paste, honey, soy sauce, malt syrup, and spices.
cranberry cranberries that have been cooked in a sugar syrup.
fish also called nam pla or nuoc nam; made from pulverized salted fermented fish, most often anchovies. Has a pungent smell and strong taste; use sparingly.
hoisin a thick, sweet, and spicy Chinese sauce made from salted fermented soy beans, onions, and garlic.
oyster Asian in origin, this rich, brown sauce is made from oysters and their brine, cooked with salt and soy sauce, and thickened with starches.

PLUM a thick, sweet and sour dipping sauce made from plums, vinegar, sugar, chilies, and spices.
satay spicy peanut sauce.
soy made from fermented soy beans. Several variations are available. We use Japanese soy sauce, an all-purpose low-sodium soy sauce, unless otherwise indicated. It is possibly the best table soy and the one to choose if you only want one variety.
light soy a fairly thin, pale but salty tasting sauce; used in dishes in which the natural color of the ingredients is to be maintained. Do not confuse with salt-reduced or low-sodium soy sauces.
sweet chili a comparatively mild, Thai-style sauce made from red chilies, sugar, garlic, and vinegar.
teriyaki a Japanese sauce made from mirin, sugar, soy sauce, ginger, and other spices.
tomato also known as ketchup or catsup; made from tomatoes, vinegar, and spices.
tomato pasta made from a blend of tomatoes, herbs, and spices.
Worcestershire thin, dark-brown spicy sauce made from tamarind, soy sauce, onions, molasses, lime, garlic, anchovies, vinegar, and seasonings.

SPECK cured smoked pork; available from delicatessens.

SPINACH soft-leaf green; good cooked or eaten raw.

STAR ANISE a dried star-shaped pod with an astringent aniseed flavor. Available both whole and ground.

SUGAR

brown an extremely soft, finely granulated sugar retaining molasses for its flavor.

confectioner's sugar also known as powdered sugar; granulated sugar crushed together with a small amount of cornstarch added.

raw brown granulated sugar.

superfine finely granulated table sugar.

white a coarse, granulated table sugar, also known as crystal sugar.

SUMAC purple-red, astringent spice ground from berries growing on shrubs that flourish wild around the Mediterranean; adds a tart, lemony flavor.

SWEET POTATO there are three types, orange sweet potato, with a sweet flavor; the white sweet potato, which has a purple flesh and an earthy flavor; and the purple sweet potato, which has a white flesh that discolors when cut and is best for baking.

SWEETENED CONDENSED MILK 60% of the water has been removed; the remaining milk is then sweetened with sugar.

TATSOI a variety of bok choy, also known as rosette bok choy. Dark leafed, it is tougher and requires longer cooking.

TOFU also known as bean curd, an off-white, custard-like product made from the "milk" of crushed soy beans; comes fresh as soft or firm. Leftover fresh tofu can be refrigerated in water (which is changed daily) for up to 4 days.

TURMERIC, GROUND also known as kamin; imparts a golden color to the dish.

VINEGAR

balsamic made from the juice of Trebbiano grapes; it is a deep rich brown color with a sweet and sour flavor.

cider (apple cider) made from fermented apples.

red wine based on fermented red wine.

sherry made from a blend of wines and left in wood vats to mature where they develop a rich mellow flavor.

white wine made from a blend of white wines.

ZUCCHINI small, pale- or dark-green, yellow or white vegetable belonging to the squash family.

index

conversion chart

Measures

All cup and spoon measurements are level. The most accurate way to measure dry ingredients is to use a spoon to fill the measuring cup, without packing or scooping with the cup, and leveling off the top with a straight edge.

When measuring liquids, use a clear glass or plastic liquid measuring cup with markings on the side.

Unless otherwise indicated, always work with room-temperature ingredients. Cold liquids added to butter can cause any batters and icings to break. We use large eggs averaging 2 ounces each.

Dry Measures

IMPERIAL	METRIC
½oz	15g
1oz	30g
2oz	60g
3oz	90g
4oz (¼lb)	125g
5oz	155g
6oz	185g
7oz	220g
8oz (½lb)	250g
9oz	280g
10oz	315g
11oz	345g
12oz (¾lb)	375g
13oz	410g
14oz	440g
15oz	470g
16oz (1lb)	500g
24oz (1½lb)	750g
32oz (2lb)	1kg

Liquid Measures

IMPERIAL	METRIC
1 fluid oz	30ml
2 fluid oz	60ml
3 fluid oz	100ml
4 fluid oz	125ml
5 fluid oz (¼ pint/1 gill)	150ml
6 fluid oz	190ml
8 fluid oz	250ml
10 fluid oz (½ pint)	300ml
16 fluid oz	500ml
20 fluid oz (1 pint)	600ml
1¾ pints	1000ml (1 liter)

Length Measures

IMPERIAL	METRIC
⅛in	3mm
¼in	6mm
½in	1cm
¾in	2cm
1in	2.5cm
2in	5cm
2½in	6cm
3in	8cm
4in	10cm
5in	13cm
6in	15cm
7in	18cm
8in	20cm
9in	23cm
10in	25cm
11in	28cm
12in (1ft)	30cm

Oven Temperatures

These oven temperatures are only a guide for conventional ovens. For convection ovens, check the manufacturer's manual.

	°F (FAHRENHEIT)	°C (CELSIUS)
Very slow	250	120
Slow	275–300	150
Moderately slow	325	160
Moderate	350–375	180
Moderately hot	400	200
Hot	425–450	220
Very hot	475	240

HEARST BOOKS
New York

An Imprint of Sterling Publishing
387 Park Avenue South
New York, NY 10016

DELISH
Elizabeth Shepard   Executive Director

Content contained in this book was originally published by ACP Magazines Limited and is reproduced with permission.

Photography by Rob Palmer
U.S. edition packaged by LightSpeed Publishing, Inc.; design by X-Height Studio
Culinary Americanization: Wes Martin

Library of Congress Catalog-in-Publication Data Available

KOHL'S
ISBN 978-1-61837-139-3
Factory Number: 123386
10/13

2 4 6 8 10 9 7 5 3 1

Delish is a registered trademark of Hearst Communications, Inc.

www.delish.com

For information about custom editions, special sales, and premium and corporate purchases, please contact Sterling Special Sales at 800-805-5489 or specialsales@sterlingpublishing.com.

Distributed in Canada by Sterling Publishing
c/o Canadian Manda Group, 165 Dufferin Street
Toronto, Ontario, Canada M6K 3H6

Manufactured in China

www.sterlingpublishing.com

This special edition was printed for Kohl's Department Stores, Inc. (for distribution on behalf of Kohl's Cares, LLC, its wholly owned subsidiary) by Hearst Books, a division of Sterling Publishing.

Sterling ISBN 978-1-61837-139-3